# Feast and Folly

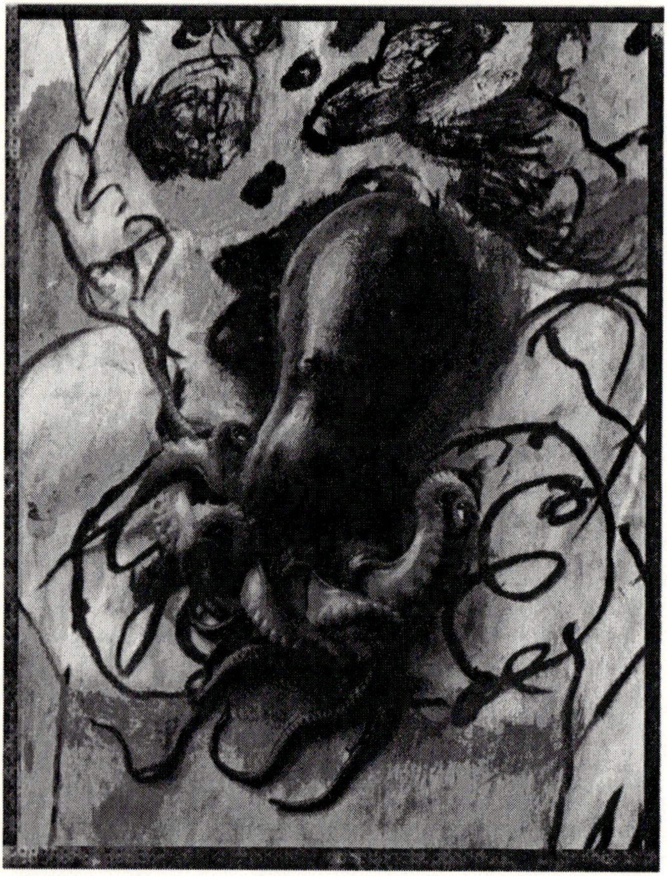

# Feast and Folly

## *Cuisine, Intoxication, and the Poetics of the Sublime*

*Allen S. Weiss*

*State University of New York Press*

THE SUNY SERIES IN
POSTMODERN CULTURE
Joseph Natoli, Editor

Cover illustration: Jean-Baptiste Simeon Chardin. *The Brioche,* also called *The Dessert.* Oil on canvas. Photo: Hervé Lewandowski. Louvre, Paris, France. Courtesy of Réunion des Musées Nationaux/Art Resource, NY.

Frontispiece by Sylvia Lachter

Published by
State University of New York Press, Albany



Printed in the United States of America



For information, address State University of New York Press, 90 State Street, Suite 700, Albany, NY 12207

Production by Dana Foote
Marketing by Fran Keneston

**Library of Congress Cataloging-in-Publication Data**

Weiss, Allen S., 1953–
Feast and folly : cuisine, intoxication, and the poetics of the sublime /
Allen S. Weiss.
p. cm.
Includes bibliographical references and index.
ISBN 0-7914-5517-3 (alk. paper) — ISBN 0-7914-5518-1 (pbk. : alk. paper)
1. Gastronomy. 2. Cookery, French. 3. Food habits—France. I. Title.

TX637 .W45 2002
641′.01′3—dc21
2002066967

10 9 8 7 6 5 4 3 2 1

*Beauty will be edible or it will no longer be.*
—Salvador Dali

*The preparation of a simple tomato is more difficult than the solution to the problem of god's infinitude.*
—Antonin Artaud

*À Porc-Épic, le Clouteur d'Oulhou.*

# Contents

# Acknowledgments

"Drunken Space" first appeared in French in *Les Cahiers du Musée national d'art moderne* (Paris, Centre Pompidou 2000), and a much shorter version will appear in Anna Alexander and Mark Roberts, eds., *High Culture* (State University of New York Press). "The Ideology of the Pot-au-feu" first appeared in Allen S. Weiss, ed., *Taste, Nostalgia* (New York, Lusitania Press, 1997); the present version is highly revised and augmented. Parts of "In the Devil's Kitchen" appeared in French in Allen S. Weiss, *Flamme et festin : Une poétique de la cuisine* (Paris, Éditions Java 1994), and in *Sulfur.* Earlier versions of "The Epic of the Cephalopod" have appeared in *Critique, Cabinet,* and in *Discourse 24:1* (Detroit, Wayne State University Press, 2002). A first version of "Tractatus Logico-Gastronomicus" was published in *Flamme et festin,* while the present revised version appeared in © 2001 *French Food: On the Table, On the Page, and in French Culture,* edited by Lawrence R. Schehr and Allen S. Weiss, reproduced by permission of Routledge, Inc., part of the Taylor & Francis Group. Some elements of "An Introduction to Modern French Cuisine through Several Exemplary Menus" were published in *Cabinet.* The passage from Antonin Artaud's "Ci-gît," translated by Clayton Eshleman with Bernard Bador, is from *Watchfiends & Rack Screams: Works from the Final Period by Antonin Artaud* (Boston, Exact Change, 1995), and is reprinted with the kind permission of the translator and publisher.

# Preface

# Transcendent or Transcendental?—Cuisine as Fine Art

*A butcher cutting, chopping, slicing, trimming, tying, is worth a dancer, a mime.*
—Colette, *Le fanal bleu*

In 1998 the French art journal *Beaux Arts* inaugurated a column on art and cuisine. This event, of little import itself, is, however, an epiphenomenon of a much larger and longstanding discursive history, one linking cuisine to the fine arts. (As this book goes to press, the curriculum of the French *lycée* is being revamped, and will henceforth include gastronomy as an integral part of the culture patrimony.) A typical statement of this position is expressed in a classic of that minor genre, the culinary novel, Marcel Rouff's *La vie et la passion de Dodin-Bouffant, gourmet* (The Life and Passion of Dodin-Bouffant, Gourmet, 1924): "Cuisine is still the victim of lowly and deplorable prejudices. Its most noble geniuses still have not conquered the right to be placed between Raphael and Beethoven . . . . [I]t would be necessary to write a huge book to maintain, through theses, counter-theses and syntheses, that the gastronomic art, like all other arts, contains a philosophy, a psychology and an ethics, that it is an integral part of universal thought, that it is tied to the civilization of our earth, to the culture of our taste, and, consequently, to the superior essence of humanity."[1] Such is the task of this book: to examine those aspects of cuisine that reach beyond the qualitatively transcendent to the metaphysically transcendental.

For the last half-millenium, especially in France, the presence of food *among* the fine arts, as well as its existence *as* a fine art, has been the subject of a continually changing history and endlessly revised debates. One of the early nodal points of the intersecting histories of art, literature, mythology, and cuisine is Francesco Colonna's Italian Renaissance fantasy, the *Hypnerotomachia Poliphili* (The Strife of Love in a Dream, 1499), an allegorical initiatory erotic drama couched in the form of a dream, presented as a vast syncretic inmixing of styles, sources, structures. This book was to have an inestimable influence on the subsequent history of European art, first in relation to the Italian Renaissance garden, and later to the seventeenth-century French formal garden and courtly festivals. In this work, cuisine played a major role in the seductions of the flesh and the elevations of the spirit. In a time when the differences between art and craft were not yet reified and hierarchized in academic discourse, the arts of the table were easily integrated into a larger setting that included all of the fine arts. The banquet scene is worth quoting at length, to give a sense of the excessive luxurience of this imaginary table.

> For the first course, all the dishes, as well as the table of the queen, were of pure gold, and we were served a cordial preserve, made, as far as I could fathom, of unicorn horn shavings, two types of sandalwood, pearls first cooked and then dissolved in spirits to form a liquid, manna, pine nuts, musk, and gold ground in rose water, all carefully mixed with sugar and starch to form a solid substance. Each of us were given two pieces without anything to drink, this being a foodstuff that protects from poison, cures fever and melancholic humors, and conserves health and youth.
>
> Forthwith the tablecloths were removed, violets were scattered all over, and at that very instant the tables were again covered with the same Persian silk in which the damsel servants were cheerfully clothed, and then strewn with orange blossoms. Then the gold table that was before the queen was removed, and in its place was set a table of beryl, with dishes of the same substance. Each of us was

presented with five little cakes or fritters with a saffroned crust, made of sugar boiled in rose water, diluted with musked water, and sprinkled with candied sugar. The first was cooked in orange flower oil, the second in clove oil, the third in jasmin oil, the fourth in benzoin oil, and the fifth in oil of amber and musk. Once sated with this savory dish, we were brought great covered bowls of beryl, upon which were placed slender napkins of gold-threaded silk, thrown over the shoulders and draped behind the damsels who bore them, falling to a half-foot above the ground. This was the manner in which all the food and drink were served. I truly believe that the wine we drank was harvested by the gods on the Elysian Fields, for it is impossible that the inhabited earth could produce so precious a liqueur. We drank to our delight.

Then the tableclothes were removed, and others of gray silk were brought forthwith, and the damsel servants, clothed in the same silk, scattered white, vermillion and pink Damask roses, serving each of us six slices of plump capon, conserved in a sauce made of fat, saffroned rose water and a bit of orange juice, along with six slices of white bread. There then appeared before our eyes another sauce, of lemon juice sweetened with sugar along with capon livers mashed with pine nuts and moistened with rose water, musk, and cinnamon. During this third course the queen's table and dishes were of topaz; once finished, the fourth course was immediately set before us, the table covered with the same beautiful yellow satin in which the damsel servants, who arrived strewing lily-of-the-valley, were also elegantly clothed. Then each of us was served seven partridge stomachs with the same number of slices of bread, whiter than milk; the sauce was made of crushed almonds, sugar, starch, yellow sandalwood, musk, and rose water extract. The queen's dishes and table were of chrysolite. For the second time we were offered the initial beverage to drink.

The fifth tablecloth was of crimson silk, like the costumes of the damsel servants; the flowers were yellow, white and violet stock. Each of us was offered eight pieces of pheasant wing and as many slices of bread. The sauce consisted of egg yolks, pine nuts, orange water, pomegranate juice, sugar, and cinnamon. The queen's dishes and table were of oriental emerald. Once this course was finished, another tablecloth was placed, of violet silk covered with jasmin flowers, like the clothes of the damsel servants. Our dish was peacock breast in a green sauce made of ground pistachios, sugar, starch, musk, thyme, wild thyme, sweet marjoram, sorrel and gilliflowers.

For the seventh and last course, before the queen was set a sumptuous ivory table, upon which was placed another of aloe wood, engraved with leaves, flowers, vases, little monsters, and small birds; the space between the two was filled with a fine paste of musk and amber. It was a magnificent masterpiece, both aromatic and exquisite to behold. The tablecloths and napkins were of Carysto silk, as were the dresses and garments of the damsels; the flowers consisted of all sorts of carnations and wallflowers. Yet who, in fact, would be able to grasp the great delicacy of such diverse and oft changing scents? The dish was of dates and pistachios crushed in rose water, with musk and sugar covered with pure gold, such that the morsels seemed to be of solid gold; each of us was offered three pieces. The dishes were of hyacinth, as was befitting the great pomp and excellence of this triumphal and divine banquet. When the tablecloths were removed, a huge, beautiful gold basin full of glowing coals was carried in, and the napkins and tablecloths were thrown into it, where they remained so long that they were entirely ablaze. They were then removed, and once cooled off, they returned to their initial state, clean and whole, as white as if they had been taken out of a sideboard just after being washed. This seemed to be a novel and marvelous thing, at least to me, who was not

> accustomed to observe such mysteries which, the more deeply I considered them, the more ignorant and bewildered I seemed to be. Nonetheless, I took great pleasure in seeing such a triumphal and prodigious expenditure, such that neither Sicilian banquets, Attalic ornaments, Corinthian vases, nor Cyprian delicacies, were anything in comparison.[2]

In this most extravagent of meals, cuisine exists *among* the other arts, as the *simulacrum of* other arts, and *as* fine art. The aesthetic sphere at this historic moment—just before modern epistemology was inaugurated and natural categories rationalized in the epoch of Descartes and Linnaeus—was all the more complex and rich due to the equivocation of ontological categories and the ostentation of stylistic admixture. Furthermore, one might note correspondences between the dishes portrayed in this feast and certain of the more adventurous inventions of our own contemporary "nouvelle" haute cuisine: indeed, the vast range of syncretism and hybridization in the *Hypnerotomachia Poliphili* makes of it a distant yet distinct precursor to the postmodern sensibility.

Such aesthetic complexity was to greatly enrich the history of French art, including that of cuisine. The first of the great festivals at Versailles under Louis XIV, on 18 July 1668, began with a feast. In *Relation de la fête de Versailles,* André Félibien, art historian and Historiographe des Bâtiments du Roi, describes the setting of this "light" meal, composed upon five grand tables set in the Bosquet de l'Étoile:

> One of these tables represented a mountain where, within several types of cavernes, diverse sorts of cold meats could be seen. The other was like the facade of a palace, constructed of marzipan and fruit jellies. It was laden with pyramides of candied fruits, another with an infinitude of vessels filled with all sorts of liqueurs, and the last was composed of caramels. All these tables, whose backboards

> were ingeniously formed into diverse compartments, were covered with an infinitude of delicate things, and presented in a wholly new manner: their feet and back panels were surrounded with foliage intermingled with festoons of flowers, one of which was supported by bacchantes. Between these tables was a small lawn of green moss leading to a pond upon which could be seen, in a huge receptacle, an orange tree bearing crystallized oranges. Alongside each of these orange trees were two other trees of different species, whose fruits were similarly crystallized.
>
> From amidst these tables arose a jet of water over thirty feet high, whose fall made a most agreeable sound. It was as if, seeing these buffets from the same height, all joined by the tree branches and flowers with which they were adorned, it were a small mountain from the heights of which emerged a fountain.[3]

Furthermore, as if offered as the very allegory of the feast itself (or, perhaps, simply as an incitation to sensual license), the evening also included a musical comedy by Molière and Lully, *Fêtes d'Amour et de Bacchus,* interspersed with the contrasting though hardly anthithetical claims by Amour, "Oh, what pleasure to love!" and by Bacchus, "Oh, what pleasure to drink!" The moral of the tale is that the two gods must not be separated—a conclusion that certainly inspired the libertine *petits soupers* of the Regency, but one that would subsequently be vigorously contested at the very moment of the birth of a modern, more bourgeois and democratic (and therefore more sedate and equilibrious) gastronomy around 1800.

Félibien's descriptions of the great festivals at Versailles reveal the profoundly poetic construction, narrative continuity, and aesthetic coherence of these events. It is evident that these festivals are indeed consummate compositions, combining ballet, theater, music, feasts, fireworks, waterworks, and illuminations into a total work of art. This aesthetic totality is celebrated and allegorized by the fireworks that culminated the fifth day of the festival of 1674, as described by Félibien in *Les Divertissements de Versailles* (1674):

> We saw, emerging from the eyes, nostrils and muzzle of the dragon set upon the canal, a torrent of fire from which arose a thick cloud of smoke that, while being quite terrible, also revealed its own beauties. For, from its huge red and bluish clouds like those seen during great storms, there emerged a thousand thunderbolts and a thousand flashes of lightening, some describing long trails in the air, some snaking from one place to another, some first rising, to then plunge into the water, and all creating a thousand different effects. An infinite number of similar fireworks simultaneously emerged from around the canal, during which time the dragon vomited forth such a huge quantity that his muzzle seemed a chasm from which emerged a thousand enflamed sprites playing or battling together. The entirety of the water was covered by the fireworks that shot forth to the end of the canal and, after having meandered either on the surface of, or in between, the two expanses of water, they rose in little whirlwinds of fire and, making a thousand turns in the air, burst with a terrifying noise, at the same time producing an infinitude of other fires creating new effects. Everything that could be seen within the great extent of more than three hundred fathoms was neither fire nor air nor water. These elements were so completely mixed together that, being unrecognizable, a new element of a quite extraordinary nature emerged. It seemed to be composed of a thousand sparks of fire that, like a thick dust or rather an infinitude of atoms of gold, sparkled amidst an ever greater light.[4]

This spectacular pyrotechnic display, where the nearly apocalyptic dissolution of the world into flame recreated the cosmos at a higher level of existence, not only symbolized the cosmogonic powers of the Sun King, but also served as an allegory for the festival in which it was couched. For it is not the opera—with its stage strictly limited in space and its representations limited in time—that is the ultimate avatar of such a totalizing project. Rather, the garden constitutes the site of the original *Gesamtkunstwerk,* for the garden is both spectacle and stage, existing simultaneously as an artwork in itself and as the site for the representation, conjunction, and synthesis of all the arts. To rethink the garden in this manner—increasingly polymorphic, polyvalent, equivocal—reveals its role as the unstated *site of heterogeneity itself,* as the synthesizing *site of all sites and all arts* (including that of cuisine, as is attested to by the role of the feasts at Versailles). Félibien constantly reminds us that the garden is not merely a visual spectacle, and that the poetic logic of the landscape necessitates and instantiates a synaesthetic inmixing of all the senses, guided by a specific, highly symbolized use-value, and culminating in an aesthetic experience that is greater than the sum of its sensory, sensual, symbolic, and historic parts. This richer experience of the garden—combining art and magic, fascination and observation, history and mythology—offers a model for understanding the inextricable intermingling of all the arts.[5] Though the hierarchized system of fine arts that was being established by the Académie Royale de Peinture et de Sculpture, founded in Paris in 1648, would hold no place for gastronomy and the "arts of the table," the amalgamation of the arts in the great festivals established, however, a de facto aesthetic ensemble that provided the context for, even if not yet the reality of, the integration of cuisine into the nascent system of the *beaux arts.* This opportunity, missed by seventeenth-century theorists, would not be lost on future gastronomes.

One of the earliest French references to cuisine as a fine art, simile aside, is to be found in the preface, written by two Jesuits, Guillaume-Hyacinthe Bougeant and Pierre Brumoy, to the classic cookbook, *Dons de Comus* (1739): "Cuisine, like all the other Arts invented out of need or pleasure, was perfected through the Genius of the people, and it has become more delicate to the extent that it has been refined. In the civilized Nations, the progress of cuisine followed that of all the other arts."[6] As was most often the case in the eighteenth-century—where the notion of art was in the process of being radically modified and expanded—such proclamations reveal a cognitive slippage in the use of the term *art*, ambiguously signifying something between "art" and "craft." Such considerations were further examined in Étienne-Laureault de Foncemagne's preface, entitled "Dissertation préliminaire sur la cuisine moderne," to Menon's cookbook *La Science du maître d'hôtel cuisinier* (1749), a veritable treatise of aesthetics in which the former asserts, unambiguously, that cuisine is an art just like poetry, music, and painting.[7] Just as the *literary* and *practical* conditions for considering cuisine as existing among the fine arts were already established in the seventeenth-century court festivals, these Enlightenment thoughts inaugurated the *conceptual* and *aesthetic* preconditions for the new "art" of cuisine. Soon afterward, the revolution, despite itself, created the *material* and *discursive* preconditions for a new cuisine, as new sources of patronage and creativity were established at the dawn of the nineteenth-century. The restaurant was born, and it is here that the history of modern French cuisine begins.

The very term *gastronomy* began to circulate around 1801, with the first verified instance occuring in a poem by Joseph de Berchoux, "La Gastronomie, ou l'Homme des champs à table." Simultaneously, a new literary genre emerged, that of gastronomic writing—which often took for granted that cuisine exists among the fine arts—inaugurated by Alexandre-Balthazar-Laurent Grimod de la Reynière's *Almanach des gourmands* (1803) and *Manuel des Amphitryons* (1808).[8] Subsequently, Jean-Anthelme Brillat-Savarin paradoxically proclaims in *Physiologie du goût* (*The Physiology of Taste;* 1826), one of the foundational texts of modern French gastronomy, both that "cuisine is the most ancient art," and "Gasterea is the tenth muse: she presides over the joys of taste."[9] Is the term *art* used metaphorically? Are these aesthetically hyperbolic, and perhaps slightly tongue-in-cheek, statements mere expressions of an impassioned gourmet for whom cooking and eating are necessarily arts sine qua non? Or does Brillat-Savarin imply that cuisine was a craft recently raised to the level of art, no doubt in great part by his very own writings? Whether this apparent contradiction—of cuisine as simultaneously the oldest and the most recent art—reveals an ambiguity regarding the aesthetic status of cuisine, or rather a verity about its newfound social status, in either case it occurs at a historic juncture which was to mark the origins of modern French haute cuisine.

While modernist aesthetics was fundamentally based on the analysis of relatively stable formal characteristics of art works, postmodern hermeneutics has incorporated the "anxious" nature of much late twentieth-century art. The result is that contemporary aesthetic discourse is not primarily a function of formal qualities, but of intersecting (and often contradictory) discursive networks—a complex strategy necessary in a field of multi-, mixed-, inter-, and hyper-media, and in a world of increasing stylistic hybridization, technical simulation, and global authorial interchange. Among the results of this new aesthetics is the disappearance of the boundaries between the arts, the breakdown of the border between art and craft, the questioning of classic hierarchies of form and taste, and the expansion of what constitutes the aesthetic field. One example of these transformations that has recently received much attention is the question of whether fashion is a fine art; these arguments, mutatis mutandis, also obtain for cuisine and gastronomy. In "Is Fashion Art?," Sung Bok Kim analyzes the manner in which fashion criticism is aesthetically grounded, revealing how it is akin to art criticism. She utilizes James D. Carney's "style-relative model of art criticism"[10] to investigate the epistemology of the field of fashion writing, enriching her analysis with Wittgensteinian considerations gleaned from the works of Arthur Danto, who explains that, "to see something as art requires something the eye cannot decry—an atmosphere of artistic theory, a knowledge of the history of art: an art-world."[11] Valorizing a theory of art "compatible with the open disjunctive concept of art (whereby a family resemblance is sought within the context of art history),"[12] Sung Bok Kim investigates a network of historically situated critical and theoretical elements and activities that intersect and overlap to determine the "arthood" of a certain class of objects in the postmodern world: Locate the Style, Descriptive Features and Structures, Primary Aesthetic Features, Value Features, Low-level Interpretation, High-level Interpretation, Critical Judgment. She concludes, within this context, that given the fact that the respective discourses of contemporary art and fashion share many of the same features (and often appear in the same journals and magazines), both art and fashion enrich human experience in much the same way. Fashion has not only infiltrated the discourse of the fine arts, but one could extrapolate and suggest that it has finally been admitted into the system of the *beaux arts*.

Much the same can be said for cuisine. In a recent text that goes far to clarify many longstanding ambiguities about the aesthetic status of cuisine—as well as to explain why it is specifically French cuisine that most often serves as the subject of European and American gastronomic discourse—Priscilla Parkhurst Ferguson offers a sociologically based analysis of the social, economic, and cultural conditions that shaped the culinary-gastronomic domain in nineteenth-century France. The main elements of this field contain:

> First, abundant, various, and readily available foodstuffs; second, a cadre of experienced producers (chefs) in a culturally specific site (the restaurant), both of which are supported by knowledgeable, affluent consumers (diners); and third, a secular cultural (culinary) tradition. All of these

> elements—the food, the people and places, the attitudes and ideas—came together in early 19th-century France with a force hitherto unknown and, indeed, unsuspected.[13]

Parallel to Sung Bok Kim's analysis in regard to fashion, Priscilla Parkhurst Ferguson explains that cuisine indeed exists as an aesthetic phenomenon, due to the attributes it shares with the other arts. This popularization, valorization, and aestheticization of cuisine was fortified by the longstanding existence of Paris as the cultural center of France, underpinned by a concomitant communality of educational foundations in the *grandes écoles;* both of these conditions contributed to the intersection and convergence of artistic individuals, aesthetic fields, and cultural institutions.

Ferguson cites five major factors in the nineteenth century that contributed to the aestheticization of gastronomy:

> First, new social and cultural conditions stimulated production, sustained broad social participation, and encouraged a general cultural enthusiasm for the product in question. Second, specific sites came to be dedicated to cultural production and consumption. Third, the institution of standards and models of authority ensured an acute critical consciousness that focused and checked yet also legitimized the expressions of cultural excitement. Fourth, subfields generated by continued expansion of the field assured the simultaneous concord and conflict of the parties involved, the consonance and dissonance of new positions and alliances. The resulting interlocking networks of individuals and institutions forged links with adjacent fields, and it is these linkages that were largely responsible for the social prestige of gastronomy.[14]

She goes on to cite the five genres of gastronomic writing that resulted from, and answered to, the above conditions: 1. *gas-*

*tronomic journalism,* founded by Grimod de la Reynière; 2. *culinary treatises,* brought to a new level of precision, sophistication, and encyclopedism by Antonin Carême; 3. *cultural commentary,* widely popularized by Brillat-Savarin; 4. *political philosophy,* where gastronomy played a major role in the writings of Charles Fourier; 5. *literature,* revealing hitherto untold gastronomic details and scenarios, notably in the novels of Honoré de Balzac.[15] The growing popularity and prestige of these discourses, contemporaneous with the relative democratization of restaurant dining and the increased distribution of wealth in the nineteenth-century, offered the conditions for the possibility of considering cuisine as one of the fine arts.

The present study is neither a history nor a sociology of modern French cuisine, but rather an exploration of the conceptual preconditions, the discursive limits, and the poetic and rhetorical forms of the culinary imagination. It is therefore concerned, to a great extent, with what was repressed, sacrificed, abjected in order to found the discourse of a new art form. As is usually the case, the terms that underlie the expressions of an artistic practice and its critical discourse are not necessarily—indeed, are most often necessarily *not*—part of that discourse. I thus seek the points of breakdown, rupture, and nonsense, the thresholds, transgressions, and excesses, at the margins of the various genres of mainstream gastronomic writing. As such, this study has a triple purpose: to analyze the structural preconditions for considering cuisine as a fine art; to connect the diverse discursive conditions that give meaning to the notion of cuisine as artwork; and finally, to investigate the most extreme psychological and metaphysical condition of the aesthetic domain, the sublime, in relation to gastronomy. In a word, it is the relation of culinary discourse to the *sublime*—an essential topic hitherto suppressed in gastronomy and philosophy—that serves as the articulation of these essays.

The intersecting discursive fields that constitute the symbolic matrix informing this work are: 1. *metaphysics:* "Drunken Space" analyzes the modes of intoxication that have, from the ancient Greeks through Rabelais, Baudelaire, and Nietzsche, subtended both literary and culinary enterprises; 2. *sociology:* "The Ideology of the Pot-au-feu" charts the political peregrinations and symbolic reversals of a national dish; 3. *psychology:* "In the Devil's Kitchen" examines the dark underside of gastronomy, where magic and madness disturb the biological and literary processes of ingestion; 4. *literature:* "The Epic of the Cephalopod" proffers an analysis of one of the most profound novels ever centered on food; 5. *autobiography:* "Tractatus Logico-Gastronomicus" is my own "taste test," intended as a practical gauge to reveal precisely who, gastronomically, is speaking in this book. Finally, as a postface, "An Introduction to Modern French Cuisine through Several Exemplary Menus" offers an annotated selection of famous meals that mark the history of modern gastronomy, whether in culinary, sociological, or symbolic terms.

However, in a postmodern world where the prestige of "art" is diminished and the question of the "fine" arts is nearly an anachronism, of what use are such matters? Quite simply, just as "knowledge is power," it is also true that knowledge is pleasure. Here, I would hope to make some small contribution to both the pleasures of the text and the pleasures of the table—especially where the two are most intimately related. With that in mind, I would like to conclude with a citation from Gaston Bachelard's *La psychanalyse du feu* (The Psychoanalysis of Fire), a passage inspired by his childhood reminiscences of eating a waffle cooked in the open flames of the family fireplace:

> Yes, I ate fire, I ate its goldness, its aroma and even its sparkle as the burning hot waffle crunched between my teeth. And it's always like this, through a sort of enjoyment of luxuries, such as dessert, that fire reveals its humanity. It doesn't confine itself to cooking: it makes crisp. It gilds the

> crust. It materializes men's feasts. As far back as one goes, gastronomic value surpassed alimentary value, and it is in joy rather than in need that man discovered his spirit. The conquest of the superfluous offers greater spiritual excitation than the conquest of necessity. Man is a creation of desire, not a creation of need.[16]

The foundation of gastronomy is an aesthetic of excess; the pleasures of the text can only increase the joys of eating.

# 1
# Drunken Space

*Wine is truly a* universal *that knows how to make itself* singular, *but only if it finds a philosopher who knows how to drink.*
—Gaston Bachelard, *La terre et les rêveries du repos*

Moderation is often presented as one of the ideals of gastronomy. Writing of the origins of modern gastronomy, Grimod de la Reynière's *Almanach des gourmands* (1803) and *Manuel des Amphitryons* (1808), Jean-Claude Bonnet explains, "More than providing culinary information, Grimod applied himself to creating a culinary style that associated gastronomy and writing. This gourmet literature comprises a literary genre, perverse writing, and a staging of the artist, for according to Grimod, the gourmet is simultaneously a scholar, a libertine, and an aesthete."[1] This melange of scholarship, libertinage, and culinary aestheticism indeed suggested a new gastronomic imperative. However, even if, as Bonnet rightly suggests, "the sexual metaphor is a semantic operative" in Grimod, and even if "Grimod realizes all the possible commutations between the erotic and the gastronomic,"[2] a certain psychological equilibrium is necessary for all three aspects of the gastronomic art to function properly. Drunken debauchery is excluded, for it would obviate the scholarly, literary, and aesthetic aspects of the experience. Grimod was to codify, in the *Manuel des Amphitryons,* the "elements of politesse" that would guide the emerging bourgeoisie in its table manners and culinary experiences. Note the "eight qualities indispensable to the formation of a fine epicure: fortune, taste, an innate sense of good food, a penchant for munificence, love of order, gracious manners, amenity of heart, and attractiveness of spirit."[3] From these qualities would be derived a strict code of civility at table, one that would regulate specific means of serving and tasting food and wine. Needless to say, this was not a discourse of drunkenness, excess, and transgression, but of appreciation, moderation, and conviviality.

Following on Grimod's foundations, one of the aphorisms that opens Jean-Anthelme Brillat-Savarin's famous *Physiologie du goût* (1825) is, "Whoever causes himself indigestion or drunkenness does not know how to eat or drink."[4] Indeed, Brillat-Savarin distinguishes the pleasures of eating as such from the pleasures of the table: while the former entail the satiety of the sensual, animal part of man, the latter constitute a civilized experience, that of "considered sensation [*sensation réfléchie*]."[5] In his introduction to the *Physiologie du goût,* Roland Barthes explains how for Brillat-Savarin the significance of this new form of hedonism—gastronomic pleasure—is overdetermined, stemming from several causes; these are organized according to a system of conviviality (a new form of reunion), at the core of which exists, "communication as a pleasure *[jouissance]*—and not as a function."[6] Culinary pleasure is not mere excitation, but, as Grimod already insisted, it is taste as reflected and shaped by culture and ensconced in conversation and writing. As such, for Brillat-Savarin wine has no particular gastronomic privilege, much less an intoxicating role; it is an integral part of the meal, and should in no way lead to ecstasy or paroxysm. Rather, it has the function of rendering the body "brilliant," amplifying the conviviality and sociability that establishes the coherence of the group dining at table, and consequently ameliorating conversation, the very basis of the gastronomic genre. Barthes continues his analysis to reveal how Brillat-Savarin (and Barthes himself) inscribes gastronomy within discourse: "Conversation (among several) is, as it were, the law that saves culinary pleasure from all psychotic risk and keeps the gourmet in a 'healthy' rationality: by speaking, by chatting while he eats, the guest confirms his ego and protects himself from all subjective dispersion, through the imaginary of discourse."[7] Wine, in this scenario, is a conductor of reasoned conversation; its role is not that of an intoxicant, but of an "antidrug."

It is no wonder that Baudelaire begins *Paradis artificiels* (Artificial Paradises) with a scathing critique of Brillat-Savarin—whom he characterizes as an "insipid brioche," suggested by the pastry named after him[8]—noting that nothing whatsoever is to be found on the topic of wine in the *Physiologie du goût,* other than the meager information that wine is an alcoholic drink and that Noah is known as its inventor. For Baudelaire, to the contrary, in Barthes's words, "wine is remembrance and forgetting, joy and melancholy; it is what permits the subject to be transported outside of himself, to make the consistency of his ego cede in favor of strange, foreign and uprooted states; it is the path of deviance; in short, it is a drug."[9] As was already apparent in "Le vin" (Wine) a section of *Les fleurs du mal* (Flowers of Evil), intoxication through wine is acknowledged as a savior of modern humanity, as is also thematized in *Paradis artificiels:*

> The profound joys of wine, who amongst you has not known them? Whosoever has had a remorse to appease, a memory to evoke, a pain to drown, a chateau in Spain to build, you have all finally invoked it, mysterious god hidden in the fibers of the vine. How great are the spectacles of wine, illuminated by the inner sun! How true and burning is that second youth that man draws from it! But also how formidable are its overwhelming delights and its enervating enchantments.[10]

The virtue of wine, according to Baudelaire, is not only that it leads to an increase of volition, which constitutes the essence of humankind and the source of artistic creativity; furthermore, intoxication opens the gates of those artificial paradises where "we flutter toward infinity,"[11] inducing a state of the "hyper-sublime."[12] Indeed, in "Hymne à la beauté" (Hymn to Beauty) one of the early poems from *Les fleurs du mal,* Baudelaire directly compares the effects of beauty and of wine, both of which are offered as means of salvation; no matter whether it arises from heaven or hell, the crucial task is to render "the universe less hideous and the present less weighty."[13] It is as if wine and poetry existed on the same moral, aesthetic, and epistemological levels.

And yet, Baudelaire's was not an unconditional valorization of intoxication: to the salutary effects of wine (ones however no longer accepted as totally valid by our medical establishment) he opposed the destructive effects of hashish and opium. Though the latter two also permit an indulgence in the "taste for infinity," he argues that "[w]ine exalts the will, hashish annihilates it. Wine is a psychic support, hashish is a weapon for suicide. Wine renders one pleasant and sociable. Hashish isolates . . . What use is it, in fact, to work, labor, write, produce anything whatsoever, when one can find paradise in an instant? . . . Wine is useful, it produces fruitful results. Hashish is useless and dangerous."[14] Both hashish and opium create an "artificial ideal," a dreamlike state, subjugating the will and diminishing freedom, offering a joy that is none other than a solipsistic aggrandizement of the self, a vain "enlarging mirror"[15] that creates the subjective illusion of a "man-god."[16] Such intoxication is a fruitless, suicidal addiction in which the subject "rushes, from day to day, toward the luminous abyss where he admires his face of Narcissus."[17]

While the ethical implications of hashish and opium suffer Baudelaire's reprobation, the aesthetic valorization of these drugs, along with that of wine, follows that of the Romantics, for whom a decided "taste for infinity" was crucial to their art. To these transfigurations of paradise Baudelaire added the aesthetic complexities of synaesthetic correspondences; in hashish hallucinations, for example, "The most singular equivocations, the most inexplicable transpositions of ideas take place. Sounds have a color, colors have a music. Musical notes are numbers . . ."[18] Indeed, under the effects of such forms of intoxication, the entire aesthetic operation of the psyche seems to be excited to new heights; for example, "Grammar, arid grammar itself, becomes something like an evocatory sorcery; words resuscitate the substantif in its substantial majesty, dressed in flesh and bone; the adjective, that transparent garment that clothes and colors it like a glaze; and the verb, that angel of movement, which gives the sentence its motion."[19] In their formal effects, such intoxicants create, or at least duplicate, the system of correspondences at the core of Baudelaire's aesthetic. Compare his lighthearted celebration of wine (which seems to prefigure the specialization of today's "designer drugs"):

> I open the *Kreisleriana* of the divine Hoffmann, and I read a curious recommendation. The conscientious musician must partake of Champagne in order to compose a comic opera. He shall find a frothy gayness therein. Religious music necessitates wines of the Rhine or Jurançon. They contain an inebriating bitterness, as in the depths of profound ideas; but heroic music cannot do without Burgandies. They contain the serious fire and the drive of patriotism.[20]

These considerations would come to sustain one of the great aesthetic encounters of modernity.

Baudelaire records his aesthetic shock in discovering Wagner's music, in a letter addressed to the musician dated 17 February 1860 (the year of publication of *Paradis artificiels*), concerning selections from *Tannhäuser* and *Lohengrin:* "Generally, these profound harmonies appear to resemble those stimulants that accelerate the pulse of the imagination," inciting sensations that he characterizes as hyperbolically as possible, specifically described as "the supreme scream of the soul brought to paroxysm."[21] In the heat of enthusiasm, Baudelaire's praise characterizes his own emotive state better than it describes the structure of the music, and one might well ask which sorts of stimulants he refers to in this letter.

Rectification is given a year later, in his lengthy and detailed analysis, "Richard Wagner et *Tannhäuser* à Paris," in a paragraph that simultaneously epitomizes the intoxicating nature of aesthetics, the concern with the "coincidence of several arts,"[22] and the issue of correspondences or synaesthesia:

> No musician excels Wagner in *painting,* materially and spiritually, both space and depth. . . . He possesses the art of translating, by subtle gradations, everything that is excessive, immense, and ambitious in spiritual and natural man. It sometimes seems, while listening to this ardent and despotic music, that one rediscovers the vertiginous conceptions of opium, painted on a background of shadows and torn apart by reverie.[23]

Baudelaire intercalates into the critical text several lines from his poem "Correspondances," as a reminder that "God proffered the world as a complex and indivisible totality."[24] These are not metaphors, but rather the overture to a new epistemology and aesthetics. In a rhetoric that prefigures that of Nietzsche's *Thus Spoke Zarathustra,* Baudelaire writes of the emotions invoked by Wagner's art: "I felt delivered from the bonds of *weightiness,* and I found through memory the extraordinary *voluptuousness* that circulates in high places,"[25] a stimulating, inspiring condition of lightness celebrating all that is implied by "*will, desire, concentration, nervous intensity, explosion.*"[26] Wine, opium, and a certain music create an ecstatic temporality that overcomes the quotidian irreversibility of time and the partition of the senses; henceforth, art is no longer a function of expressing states of the soul, but rather of creating metamorphoses, establishing correspondences, seeking infinity.[27] Consequently, Baudelaire stressed a quest for the absolute: "Every well-formed brain bears within itself two infinities, heaven and hell, and it immediately recognizes half of itself in every image of either of these infinities."[28] This claim is certainly not without a certain quotient of Pascalian anguish; indeed, the theological is always on the horizon of Baudelaire's work, and one of his attractions to *Lohengrin* was that it evoked, "the craving of the spirit for the incommunicable God."[29] However, while the dual infinities of Pascalian theology are objectively external and theologically determinant, for Baudelaire heaven and hell—invoked and nourished by "infinite melodies" mysteriously arising from invisible orchestras—are subjectively innate and psychologically disquieting. The antipodes of the soul are joined at the border between intoxication and delirium: joy and morbidity, rapture and oblivion, all coalesce in an intuition that eliminates time and transforms space, the very forms of consciousness.

It is precisely at this point, through the "artificial paradises" of intoxication and music, that temporal contradictions vanish in an eternal moment of reversibility; spatial contradictions disappear from the point of view of infinity; and the divisions of the senses are overcome through synaesthesia. But this is hardly Romantic mysticism, and the implications for aesthetics are contemporary and unique, as Gaston Bachelard points out, stressing that the Baudelairian theory of correspondences is operative only on condition of "a pullulating and audacious sensualism, drunk with inexactitude."[30] This epistemology—indeed one of intoxication, where the real and the ideal exist in disturbing promiscuity—operates in diametrical opposition to the sensualist tradition of Locke and Condillac. Baudelaire's theory of correspondences—where the ideal is compelled to excite all the senses—is one of polyvalence and reciprocity, entailing a sensorial metaphoricity irreducible to sheer sense data. Bachelard elaborates:

> The sensations are hardly any longer the occasional causes of isolated images. The *real cause of the flux of images* is truly the *imagined cause* . . . . [T]he *function of the unreal* is the

> function that truly drives the psychic mechanism, while the *function of the real* is one of blockage, of inhibition, a function that *reduces* images in such a manner as to give them the simple value of a sign. It is clear that the immediate *contributions* of the imagination must be considered alongside the immediate *givens* of sensation.[31]

Realism and classicism are subverted by an influx of Romantic idealism, where the quotidian and the contingent are interiorized as a system of symbols, and perception is produced autonomously by the psychic mechanism. Like alcohol, such correspondences attenuate the inhibitions imposed by the reality principle, establishing new ratios and relations between the senses; as Bachelard astutely remarks, writing specifically of the effects of wine, "Contradictions that would be intolerable in their initial sensible state come alive through a transposition into another sense."[32] This is hardly a Hegelian dialectical reconciliation of opposites, but rather the celebration of an aesthetics of inexactitude, an epistemology of perpetual poesis, slippage, transfer, metamorphosis, deviation, *drunkenness.*

In all these states of intoxication, whether inspiring or stultifying, spectacle is reduced to illusion or delusion; perception is increasingly mobile; the sense of self expanded; the apparent structure of the world destabilized. Seeking the ultimate extrapolation of Romantic aesthetics, an iconoclastic technique of theaterless theater is suggested, one that effects a *counter-memory, counter-spectacle,* and *counter-symbolic.* The very body of the observer becomes theater. This new technique of scenarization is coherent with the physiological experimentation and theorization of the nineteenth century, which came to understand perception to be possible in a nonreferential manner.[33] Such was demonstrated by experiments proving that the body may produce phenomena without any external correlates, by mechanical, electrical, and chemical means: a single stimulus may have diverse effects, and different stimuli may have similar effects. For example, the study of visual after-images and hypnagogic images, divorced from direct visual perception, reveal them to often be strikingly homologous to a sort of inner fireworks. In his study of this scientific paradigm shift, Jonathan Crary, in *Techniques of the Observer,* concludes that "[t]he very absence of referentiality is the ground on which new instrumental techniques will construct for an observer a new 'real' world."[34] Such is the reality of Baudelaire's drug-induced artificial paradises. To seek the aesthetic limits of such physiological effects and scientific techniques would be to theorize not the sublime but the countersublime, where temporality is constituted by a reflexivity closed in upon physiological rhythms and thresholds; where consciousness, subsumed by pure presence, eschews all transcendence; where the imagination exists in direct proportion to somatization; and where, purged of language, the symbolic codes are abolished. Narration is obliterated, time nullified, and the psychic mechanism thrust into a solipsism rivaling that of the mystics, inaugurating the oxymoron of an innate apocalyptic sublime.

This interiorization of perception—the implosion of the senses into a unified source of creative intuition (often aided by sundry modes of intoxication)—was exemplified by the contemporary disintegration of the division between senses, genres, and arts: 1. Baudelaire's notion of correspondences offered a new aesthetic paradigm, whereby "the *imagination* is the most *scientific* of the faculties, because it alone understands *universal analogy,* or what a mystical religion terms the *correspondence*";[35] 2. Wagner's operatic Gesamtkunstwerk was the culmination of the genre of the total work of art, combining all the arts in a unified scene; 3. investigations of synaesthesia abounded in the scientific literature, such that experiments were even considered to cross-connect nerves in order to permit the subject to see sounds and hear colors;[36] 4. literary hybridization became common practice, and new life was given to the ancient genre of the encyclopedic form or "anatomy," as Northrop Frye later termed it, that heterogeneous literary form which includes all forms (already reconceived by Romantic theorization), where the very notion of genres begins to disintegrate from within.[37] Referentiality and representation were no longer structural preconditions of artistic production.

However, intuitions of expanded consciousness and novel styles did not always serve Baudelaire's cause; culinary and landscape metaphors abound in this epoch, and were occasionally put to particularly acerbic use against Baudelaire. Consider the vitriolic attack in the form of a recipe, directed against *Les fleurs du mal,* that appeared in *Le Figaro* four years after the infamous trial of 1857: "Cut open a gamy and already decomposing cadaver, stuff it with well turned verse and eccentricities in as many parts as you can, dust it with paradoxes, dress it with Flowers of evil, and serve it very stiff."[38] Consider also the article written by Sainte-Beuve, in *Le Constitutionnel* of 20 January 1862, entitled "Des prochaines élections à l'Académie," concerning Baudelaire's tragicomic candidacy for the Académie Française:

> . . . in short, M. Baudelaire has found the means of building himself, at the end of a peninsula which is said to be uninhabitable, and beyond the bounds of known romanticism, a bizarre kiosk, very ornate, very overdone, but elegant and mysterious: a kiosk in which one grows drunk on abominable drugs in cups of exquisite porcelain. This singular kiosk, made of marquetry, of a deliberate and composite originality, which, for some time, has drawn people's eyes to the furthermost extremity of the romantic Kamchatka, is what I call *the Baudelaire folly.*[39]

With its distinctly appropriate evocation of Poe, this evaluation is telling. Not only is the double entendre of the word *folly* (madness and garden folly) of particular interest in this regard, but the very use of puns, mixed metaphors, and allegories takes on a new and poignant meaning in the context of the complex intermingling of senses and genres in this epoch, usages whose profundity was fully revealed at the turn of the century in Freud's *The Interpretation of Dreams.*

The aesthetic celebration of intoxication and the subsequent inmixing of the senses would find its most celebrated poetic statement in Rimbaud's claim, in a letter of 1871, that the poet must, "arrive at the unknown through the disordering of *all the senses.*"[40] That same year, Nietzsche wrote *The Birth of Tragedy,* where, inspired by Wagnerian opera, he interprets classic Greek tragedy according to the mythopoeic differentiation between the Apollonian and the Dionysian, respectively conceived as "the separate art worlds of dreams and intoxication,"[41] domains ruled by the gods of form and excess. In the state of Dionysian frenzy—where the symbolic faculties are excited to their fullest extent—the *principium individuationis* (the principle of self-identity) disintegrates, revealing the terrors and ecstasies of existence, thus entailing precisely the "psychotic risks" and "subjective dispersion" of which Barthes warned. The function of Greek tragic drama is to transform Dionysian intoxication into Apollonian vision, to transform libido into sign. Such is the foundation of a new aesthetic phenomenon:

> The essence of nature is now to be expressed symbolically; we need a new world of symbols; and the entire symbolism of the body is called into play, not the mere symbolism of the lips, face, and speech but the whole pantomime of dancing, forcing every member into rhythmic movement. Then the other symbolic powers suddenly press forward, particularly those of music, in rhythmics, dynamics, and harmony.[42]

Whereas in *The Birth of Tragedy* the dualism is such that Apollo creates a hallucinatory world of visions to veil the primal chaos represented by Dionysus, in Nietzsche's later works Apollo is subsumed within Dionysus, such that, as Nietzsche already suggests in *The Birth of Tragedy,* Dionysian states entail self-oblivion, where "*excess* revealed itself as truth."[43] Such Dionysian intoxication implies a principle of nonrepresentation—ruled by force, not form—which not only supported a profound reinterpretation of Greek tragedy, but also suggested a radical transformation of modern art and aesthetics. The end of metaphysics is prefigured by a drunken *diasparagmos,* by the ritual murder, dismemberment, and eating of the ancient god. Indeed, *in vino veritas.*

Subsequently, the ultimate metaphysical justification of intoxication was expressed in Nietzsche's *Twilight of the Idols* in terms of the psychology of the artist, specifically through the integration of the form giving Apollonian into the energy providing Dionysian aspects of the soul:

> *Toward a psychology of the artist.* If there is to be art, if there is to be any aesthetic doing and seeing, one physiological condition is indispensible: frenzy. Frenzy must first have enhanced the excitability of the whole machine; else there is no art. All kinds of frenzy, however diversely conditioned, have the strength to accomplish this: above all, the frenzy of sexual excitement, this most ancient and original form of frenzy. Also the frenzy that follows all great cravings, all strong affects; the frenzy of feasts, contests, feats of daring, victory, all extreme movement; the frenzy of cruelty; the frenzy in destruction; the frenzy under certain meteorological influences, as for example the frenzy of spring; or under the influence of narcotics; and finally the frenzy of will, the frenzy of an overcharged and swollen will.[44]

Though sexual frenzy is given ontological preference, all sorts of frenzy are appropriate to this end, including that of feasts and narcotics (the former of which have received little comment in the vast critical literature on Nietzsche), and notably that of volition, also the key to Baudelaire's psychology of the artist. The goals are the enrichment of the world through the artist's volition and fullness; the idealization and perfection of existence; the transformation of the self into a work of art; and the overcoming of Time and its terrible restrictions.

> To redeem those who lived in the past and to recreate all "it was" into a "thus I willed it"—that alone should I call redemption. . . . "It was"—that is the name of the will's gnashing of teeth and most secret melancholy. Powerless against what has been done, he is an angry spectator of all that is past. The will cannot will backwards; and that he cannot break time and time's covetousness, that is the will's loneliest melancholy. . . . That times does not run backwards, that is his wrath. . . . This, indeed this alone, is what *revenge* is: the will's ill will against time and its "it was." . . . All "it was" is a fragment, a riddle, a dreadful accident—until the creative will says to it, "But thus I willed it."[45]

Nietzsche's philosophy is consequently regulated by the hysteron-proteron, that trope which reverses the natural or dramatic order of events, thus abolishing the seemingly inexorable linearity of time. These are precisely the effects associated with Wagnerian opera. Consider Theodor Adorno's characterization of the phantasmagoria in Wagner, arguing that "the absence of any real harmonic progression becomes the phantasmagorical emblem for time standing still. . . .The standing-still of time and the complete occultation of nature by means of phantasmagoria are thus brought together in the memory of a pristine age where time is guaranteed only by stars."[46] It is in this context, for example, that "Tannhäuser mirrors the bacchanal from the remoteness of heathen prehistory on the dream stage of his own body."[47] In this eminently Nietzschean reading, the Dionysian bacchanal is represented by the Apollonian dream state: intoxication suppresses time, symbolism becomes body symbolism, and the spectator partakes in the lives of the gods.

In the penultimate chapter of *Thus Spoke Zarathustra,* "The Drunken Song," a veritable ode to joy, Zarathustra proclaims the key to his new philosophy, summed up in the sentence: "All anew, all eternally, all entangled, ensnared, enamored—oh, then you *loved* the world. Eternal ones, love it eternally and evermore; and to woe too, you say: go, but return! *For all joy wants—eternity.*"[48] Nietzsche's aesthetic of intoxication thus parallels that of Baudelaire, most succinctly expressed in one of his *Petits poèmes en prose* (Little Prose Poems): "It is time to get intoxicated! So as not to be the martyrized slaves of Time, ceaselessly intoxicate yourselves! With wine, with poetry, or with virtue, as you wish."[49] Wine is tantamount to an epistemological drug, since drunkenness entails the negation of time. Baudelaire's practice and aesthetic of intoxication, and the consequent transformations of space and time, bear striking parallels with Nietzsche's philosophy; note that for Baudelaire, in a certain aesthetic state of consciousness, "[t]his imagination endures an eternity. With a great effort, a moment of lucidity permits you to look at the clock. The eternity had lasted one minute."[50] Indeed, alas, this eternity is all too ephemeral.

In both Baudelaire and Nietzsche, we are offered the wine without the feast. It must be stressed, in gastronomic honesty and exclusive of any ad hominem arguments, that the notorious water drinker Nietzsche was far more sensitive to meteorological conditions than to wine; and that the equally notorious alcohol and opium abuser Baudelaire was often intoxicated far beyond the limits of gastronomic appreciation. These limits and dangers are both practical and metaphysical. Marcel Detienne reminds us, in *Dionysos à ciel ouvert* (Dionysius Under the Open Sky) that the people of ancient Corinth celebrated the apparition of Dionysus in his full duality by presenting, in the agora, two absolutely identical statues of gilded wood whose faces were decorated with vermillion, distinguished only by their names: *Dionysus Baccheios* and *Dionysus Lysios* or *Katharsios,* the former bringing misunderstanding, drunkenness, delirium, madness, and murder, the latter offering benevolent catharsis and purification.[51] The effects of wine are twofold, and to neglect the expiatory powers of Dionysus Katharsios is to portend the worst.

As was already made clear in terms of the social and ethical virtues of wine, it must not be forgotten, as the ancient Greeks knew all too well, that the quotidian realities of intoxication are different from its aesthetic benefits, and that there is both a qualitative and a quantitative threshold between inebriated joy and empoisonment. For while the difference between everyday drunkenness and aesthetic intoxication for Baudelaire and Nietzsche is a qualititative matter, there are also quantitative differences between degrees of intoxication, differences perhaps more astutely recognized in popular and scientific, rather than ideal, terms.

A lighthearted quantitative example of such proselytizing for temperance is the "*Thermomètre du Pochard*" (The Boozer's Thermometer), which appeared on Parisian café counters toward the end of the nineteenth century, in order to gauge six degrees of drunkenness:

1. sober *[à jeun]*
2. under way; gay *[en train; gai]*
3. going strong; moving along; tipsy *[lancé; parti; pompette]*
4. boozed; wrecked *[poivré; culotté]*
5. totaled *[compté; à son compte]*
6. round as a marble; full as an egg *[rond comme une bille; plein comme un oeuf]*.[52]

In a more literary vein, Balzac, in his *Traité des excitants modernes* (Treatise on Modern Stimulants, 1839), recounts a bet that led to a drinking bout with a friend; seventeen bottles of wine and two cigars later, the friend collapsed on a couch and

Balzac, the obvious winner, went off to the opera. He describes his experience as follows:

> What I heard of the overture of *La Gazza* equalled the fantastic sounds that fall from the heavens into the ear of a woman in ecstasy. The musical phrases reached me through brilliant clouds, stripped of all the imperfections that enter men's works, and full of all that the artist's sensibility imprinted on it of the divine. The orchestra appeared to me like a vast instrument where there occurred some sort of work whose movement and mechanism I could not grasp, as I saw most indistinctly the necks of the basses, the stirring bows, the golden curves of the trombones, the clarinettes, and the lights, but no men whatsoever. Only one or two immobile powdered heads, and two swelled, grimacing faces that disquieted me. I was half asleep.[53]

Although this description seems to prefigure Baudelaire's account of *Tannhäuser,* Balzac in fact concludes that "drunkenness is a temporary poisoning,"[54] and that physiological intoxication guarantees aesthetic deformation. For this writer, for whom coffee was the most effective literary stimulant, drunkenness is seen to be a social evil, without aesthetic recompense.

But more seriously, scientific tracts began to appear beginning at midcentury, studying the causes and effects of alcohol intoxication, though not coincidentally often studiously attempting to separate the healthful and creative effects of wine from the destructive effects of all other spirits. At the very moment that intoxication was rediscovered as a transgressive aesthetic principle, it also began to be conceived of as a public menace. The Société Française de Tempérance was founded in 1872, and on 23 January 1873 a law to suppress public drunkenness and combat alcoholism was instituted, more in response to the events of the Paris Commune than to the inflammatory statements of a Rimbaud.[55] As intoxication became central to a certain modern, indeed decadent and transgressive, aesthetics, it was simultaneously stigmatized by the powers that be. Ideal spleen and common drunkenness merged, and art was confronted with everyday reality.

Certainly, the Baudelairian revolution achieved yet another synthesis, beyond those of the senses (synaesthesia) and the arts (Gesamtkunstwerk): that of the lexical definitions of drunkenness. Consider the three major meanings of drunkenness *[ivresse]* according to the dictionary *Littré:* 1. The ensemble of phenomena determined by an excess of fermented drink, beginning with disturbances of reasoning through the state of delirium, of involuntary sleep, and even death; 2. Figurative. Disturbance produced in the soul by a passion, by a possession; 3. Poetic enthusiasm.[56] The new aesthetic of intoxication entails the *incorporation* (in the literal sense of the term) of the physical, figurative, and poetic meanings of drunkenness; the synthesis of these troubles, this enthusiasm, and this poetics of inexactitude, errancy, illusion, and perversion offers one of the epistemological foundations of a nascent modernism, where all epistemology becomes aesthesiology, a logos of the senses.[57] While Kant had shown in *The Critique of Judgment* that there are no a priori aesthetic laws, the aesthetics of intoxication in Baudelaire and Nietzsche reveal that there are also no a priori epistemological laws divorced from the corporeal symbolic, if not the negative condition of the desire to abolish the old Kantian forms of consciousness, space, and time. Baudelairian intoxication offers an ironic reversal of the Kantian sublime: for Kant, the sublime is based on the *interiorization* of infinity caused by certain terrifying aesthetic effects; for Baudelaire, this apperception of infinity now becomes a result of the *incorporation* of mind-altering drugs. Consequently, not only is a new theory of the senses offered, but a new ratio of interaction between the senses is established. As Baudelaire suggests in

*Fusées:* "*All* is number. The number is in *everything.* The number is in the individual. Drunkenness is a number."[58] Drunkenness, in this respect, follows its own laws, even if such laws now reveal the lineaments of inexactitude, indeterminacy, and the aleatory. The calculable, quantitative, isotropic coordinates of Cartesian mathematics no longer suffice to describe perception; space and time are now understood in strictly phenomenal, qualitative, heterotropic terms, describing unnatural, shifting, heterogeneous horizons of perception. Deprived of all a priori aesthetic structures, aesthetic discourse—and a fortiori the discourse of gastronomy—must henceforth be written in the first person singular; not on the basis of a subjectivization of values, but rather as a valorization of the corporeal and historical dimension of existence. Modernist poetics is determined by singularities, not laws.

A new aesthetics arose, one that finally established the preconditions for considering all the arts—including cuisine, as well as all other "crafts"—as taking part in an interlocking and nonhierarchized complex conjoining all the arts and articulated by all the senses. These conditions consist of the following:

1. The sublime is interiorized, giving rise to a corporeal sublime (an operation extrapolated from Romantic poetics);
2. Sublimation is differentiated from the sublime, such that aesthetics becomes as much a matter of desublimation as of sublimation;
3. The aesthetic field is opened to perverse libidinal cathexes (fostered by both extreme intoxication and unlimited libido);
4. Perception is conceived as a synaesthetic system (homologous with the symbolic system of correspondences), thus obviating the classic hierarchization of the senses;
5. The arts are freed from mimesis and representation;
6. The notion of the Gesamtkunstwerk authorizes the potential inmixing of forms and genres;

7. The hybridization of artistic genres is established as a paradigmatic practice.

In this originary moment of modernism, every art form now had a place (however actual, however potential) in the synaesthetic matrix; indeed, all the senses needed to be aesthetically justified and represented. Cuisine, along with the other arts—with their attendant representational, symbolic, and allegorical doubles—would now have a determined place in the formal structure of the system of the fine arts. Henceforth, cuisine too would have access to the discourse of sublimation and the sublime, as well as to the full range of free-flowing libidinal cathexes, perverse and otherwise. "Transcendent cuisine" would no longer need to seek a transcendental base in order to enter the aesthetic domain; its sensual correspondences would suffice.

This inmixing of the arts also took place in the culinary domain. Consider the following description of an early nineteenth-century *pièce montée,* as described by Grimod de la Reynière:

> Monsieur Dutfoy did not limit himself to the resources offered him by architecture; he also sought, in the art of pyrotechnics, new means of varying our pleasures. And the fireworks he adapted for his decorations, arising from amidst his palaces and temples, produced an effect easier to imagine than to describe. At the desired moment, a carefully hidden wick was lit, which burned for several minutes. Suddenly the temple was covered with odorous sparks of all colors, a thousand showers shooting to the ceiling. The guests, whose eyes and noses were simultaneously delighted *[jouissent],* stood under a vault of flamboyant sparks. The sound, the odor and the blaze of this unexpected spectacle caused a universal drunkenness, trou-

> bled by no fear of danger; for these sparks, despite their blaze, are so very innocent, that the finest fabrics were not damaged. We must admit that this sort of dessert is a veritable drama, and that it would be hard to imagine how one might end a sumptuous meal in a livelier and more dazzling manner.[59]

Already, before the post-Romantic thematizations of synaesthesia and the Gesamtkunstwerk, before the breakdown of representation and the dismantling of the boundaries between art and craft, the unlikely combination of cuisine, architecture, and pyrotechnics effected a synaesthetically organized "drama" evoking the joys of "universal drunkenness." It is as if this *pièce montée*—a footnote (or perhaps ironic pastiche) to the great *Divertissements de Versailles* and their cosmogonic fireworks, as well as being a superb prolegomena to Antonin Carême's (1783–1833) masterpieces of decorative cuisine as expressed in the forward to the third edition of his *Le Pâtissier Pittoresque* (The Picturesque Pastry Chef), where he notes the extent of his passion for architecture: "I would have ceased being a pastry chef had I blindly abandoned myself to my natural taste for the picturesque genre, such as I conceive it for the embellishment of princes' parks and private gardens."[60]—were the signal of a radical transformation of epistemic moments.

At the dawn of modernism, the synthetic and synaesthetic effects of the great seventeenth-century festivals were condensed and interiorized, first through Romanticism, and then in the light of that philosophical intoxication originating in Baudelaire, celebrated by Verlaine and Rimbaud, and theorized by Nietzsche (via Wagner) as a precondition for the end of metaphysics. The consequent transformation of aesthetics is well summed up by Bachelard: "Lyrical drunkenness no longer only appears as a parody of dionysian drunkenness."[61] As wine loosened aesthetic inhibitions and reconfigured the sensorial matrix, the realm of the senses was transformed into a bacchanal. While the nineteenth century witnessed the overt modernization and codification of French haute cuisine from Carême through Escoffier, the aesthetics of intoxication from Baudelaire through Nietzsche covertly transformed aesthetic standards and artistic forms, inaugurating a new discursive modality for cuisine that is yet to be fully theorized. Although intoxication certainly impairs the gastronomic faculties, these transgressive aesthetics—conceived in conjunction with the physiology of synaesthesia and the aesthetics of the total work of art—reconfigured the aesthetic matrix such that a potential discursive space was established that would eventually permit haute cuisine to take its place amongst the *beaux arts.* The neoclassic bacchantes that supported the garlands at the feasts of Versailles would be reincarnated as revelers in the debauched frenzy of Zarathustra's table.

# 2
# The Ideology of the Pot-au-feu

*The pot-au-feu of the people is one of the foundations of empires.*
—Comte de Mirabeau, cited in *Littré*

The very word *pot-au-feu*—pot-in-the-fire, fire-pot, the empty vessel in the flame—indicates the primal condition of cuisine, its empty form, its symbolic zero-degree of signification. Thus, the sundry poetic and political peregrinations of this dish of boiled beef and vegetables in their consommé should come as no surprise.

This tale begins several years ago, as I dined one evening at Jean-Paul Lacombe's restaurant Léon de Lyon, with Jean-Claude Bonnet, renowned specialist on Antonin Carême and Grimod de la Reynière, and with Chantal Thomas, writer and specialist in eighteenth-century literature. Jean-Claude and I both ordered, for different reasons but with equal pleasure, *Choux farcis aux truffes fraîches (ris de veau, crêtes de coq, dés de foie gras)* (stuffed cabbage with fresh truffles [sweetbreads, cockscombs, diced foie gras]). Jean-Claude chose the dish out of literary and historic curiosity, because the ingredients were those of the famed libertine suppers of the eighteenth century. I, with nostalgic glee incited by the imp of the perverse, chose the dish with the desire to compare it to one of my mother's specialties, stuffed cabbage (this being the national dish of my father's birthplace, Hungary). Both of us were thrilled, though, as may well be imagined, each of us formed quite different evaluations and nearly antithetical narratives. Chantal looked on in amazement at our desire to eat what appeared to her such a bizarre concoction, and proceeded to order a pot-au-feu. I considered this rather askance, as the most banal, traditional dish on the menu. Afterwards she insisted that it was "transubstantial." Our mutual incomprehension might well allegorize a seismic rift in the history of modern French culture.

The pot-au-feu was long considered a veritable symbol of French cuisine. (The term first appears in French in the twelfth century as *pot-a-fu,* attesting to the ancient origins of this dish.) In 1792, Goethe, while travelling in the Lorraine, dined on one, which he described as follows:

> Above the fire hung a large kettle in which the national dish, called the "pot-au-feu," was boiling. I paid attention to the preparations with much interest. The beef was already almost cooked when carrots, turnips, leeks, cabbage, and other vegetables were added. The servant placed small slices of good bread into the plates and bowls set on the table. She then poured the bouillon from the kettle and bid us to eat it. The meat and vegetables completed this very simple dinner, which seemed to please everybody.[1]

These observations are emblematic for the analysis that follows.

Claude Lévi-Strauss's analysis of the culinary triangle in *L'origine des manières de table* (The Origin of Table Manners) bears specifically on the ontology of the pot-au-feu. The opposition between the roast and the boiled entails respectively the following oppositions, all pointing to the fact that "one can place the roast on the side of nature and the boiled on the side of culture": *nonmediated* (cooked directly on an open flame) versus *mediated* (cooked in water in a closed utensil); *masculine* (open fire) versus *feminine* (protected hearth); *exo-cuisine* (cooked outside and destined for foreigners) versus *endo-cuisine* (cooked in a recipient and destined for the family or a closed group).[2] Thus, while the roast is the sort of dish offered to strangers, the boiled is one "made for intimate use and destined for a small, closed group."[3] Furthermore, the sociological markers are even more precise, insofar as "the boiled offers a method of total conservation of the meat and its juices, while the roast entails destruction or loss. One therefore evokes economy, the other prodigality; the former is of the people, the latter aristocratic."[4] Whence, "the democratic inspiration of the editors of the *Encyclopédie* is reflected in the apology they make for the boiled, 'one of man's most succulent and nourishing foods.'"[5] Not only does cuisine imply ethics (here, the "family values" of the boiled), but gastronomy becomes cosmology: "The boiled is produced without loss of substance and within an enclosed space; it is thus appropriate to symbolize cosmic totality."[6] In the most extreme expression of this symbolism, "The boiled is life, the roast death."[7]

The culinary aspects of these generalizations are borne out in terms of the foundations of modern French haute cuisine, insofar as Antonin Carême begins *L'art de la cuisine française au XIX^e siècle* (1832) with a "Traité des bouillons et potages de santé" (Treatise on Healthful Bouillons and Soups), which itself begins with an "Analyse du pot-au-feu bourgeois," followed by "Pot-au-feu de maison, ou bouillon restaurant," "Pot-au-feu au bain-marie," and "Grande marmite." His first observation is to remind us that "[t]hose men of the eighteenth century who wrote on the alimentary art didn't deign to analyse a few notions on the care that must be given to the modest pot-au-feu; however, this is the principal dish of the nation's working class."[8] He continues to situate the dish in relation to its mode of production: "It is the woman who cares after the nutritive kettle, without having the least notion of chemistry; she has simply learned from her mother the manner of attending to the pot-au-feu."[9] These considerations reveal the motivations for both the dissimulation of the pot-au-feu in the aestheticized, male-dominated domain of haute cuisine, and its resurgence in a very different, and highly moralized, milieu.

In his classic *Physiologie du goût,* Brillat-Savarin writes of the mysterious *osmazôme,* a sort of essence composed of the reduced juices of red meat. The symbolic implications of *osmazôme* are characterized by Roland Barthes in his preface to Brillat-Savarin's book:

> Faithful to his philosophy of essences, Brillat-Savarin attributes a sort of spiritual power to osmazôme. As the word is masculine, it is the very absolute of taste, a sort of meat alcohol. As a universal (demoniacal?) principle, it takes on varied and seductive appearances: it is what makes the roux of meats, the crustiness of roasts, the scent of game. And it is especially that which makes gravy and bouillon, those direct forms of quintessence (the etymology of the word goes back to the related idea of odor and bouillon).[10]

The description of this essence serves as the introduction to the very first dish listed among the specialties discussed by Brillat-Savarin, the pot-au-feu. And yet, while Brillat-Savarin emphasizes its dietary values, he immediately reveals his low estimation of this dish by describing, with the sarcasm that greatly contributed to the fame of his book, the sorts of people who enjoy eating boiled beef: people of habit, who eat it because their parents ate it, and whose children will therefore eat it; impatient people, who are always ready to jump on the first dish set before their eyes; inattentive people, who regard dining as an obligatory duty, and thus put themselves at the same level of what they eat; and finally, people of huge appetite, who simply devour their food.[11] Indeed, the critique of the pot-au-feu is based on a negative corollary derived from the notion of the consommé as essence, that is, the fact that boiled beef is the flesh minus its juice. The core of the pot-au-feu thus exists minus its essential component. Brillat-Savarin duly notes that such dishes have disappeared from fine meals.

Brillat-Savarin's critique thus sets the stage for the elimination of the pot-au-feu from the annals of haute cuisine. One may note, for example, that *Le livre de cuisine* (1867) of Jules Gouffé, student of Câreme and one of the greatest chefs of the latter part of the century, bears no mention of this dish. Escoffier—the chef who codified and collated the great recipes of the nineteenth century, those that would become the basis of French haute cuisine for nearly three-quarters of the twentieth century—would, in a curious nominal slippage, suppress this dish in his classic book, *Le guide culinaire* (1903).[12] He opens his discussion at the same point as Brillat-Savarin, for at the very beginning of his book, writing of the "Fundamental Elements of Cooking," he lists "The Principal Kinds of Fonds de Cuisine" (foundation sauces and stocks), which begins with ordinary and clarified consommés. One might thus expect that this place of honor would valorize the prime representative of the consommé, the pot-au-feu, but the fact is otherwise. For turning to recipe #599 *Pot-au-Feu,* one reads: "Prepare exactly like the petite marmite." The actual instructions are given in recipe #598 *La Petite Marmite.* In this bible of haute cuisine, the pot-au-feu is reduced to a pure name, deprived of its description, and displaced onto another recipe. This suppression is symptomatic of the direction of French gastronomy at the turn of the century, exemplified by the ascendance of Escoffier's cooking, propagated by the chain of hotels created by César Ritz, the summit of international luxury, "cosmopolitanism," and "decadence." The simple pot-au-feu, the family dish par excellence, would have little place in the complex, changing, inventive, profligate, often abstract, and occasionally absurd cuisine of the upper classes. And yet, precisely because of its traditional symbolic value and its very inappropriateness in the context of haute cuisine, the pot-au-feu would play an equally important symbolic role in the development of a reactionary literature, one that celebrates a return to the French earth and the Catholic church as the only means of salvation from a modernism whose revaluation of all values was seen by many as the ultimate catastrophe.

The text on the back cover of a recent edition of Joris-Karl Huysman's *Là-bas* (1891)—the tale of a man whose research on Gilles de Rais brings him into contact with both satanic ritual and Catholic belief—offers the following synopsis:

> Black masses and satanic invocations follow, organized by an excommunicated priest, the Canon Docre, who had the image of the cross drawn on the soles of his feet so as to constantly trample it, and whose most innocent pleasure is to feed the consecrated host to white mice. In this world of sabbaths and blasphemy, reason takes refuge in a tower of the church of Saint-Sulpice, where, for the sake of a few rare survivors, the wife of the bellringer cooks up a divine pot-au-feu.[13]

The principle theological issue at stake—the eternal battle between good and evil, as it is manifested in the contemporary French Catholic milieu—is here symbolized in culinary terms: the struggle between the life-giving principles of moral purity open to humanity, symbolized by the pot-au-feu, and the satanic traps of the Devil who, in the form of one of his avatars, the mouse, desecrates the host. The presentation of the pot-au-feu in the dining room of the belltower serves as one of the key moments of the narrative; here, one finds both a critique of modern urban culture and a celebration of the (family) values essential to the reactionary religious sentiments of the day. "This lodging was quite poor, but so very cordial, cozy, pleasant! Especially the rural table setting, the clean glasses, the dish of fresh salted butter, the jug of cider, all of which added to the intimacy of the table, lit by a slightly worn lamp that spread its tarnished silver gleam on the coarse tablecloth."[14] The simple, healthful, pure pleasures of the countryside are transported into a sacred urban space, a site of repose and communion within an otherwise fallen city. In this microcosm, even the presence of lamplight, in an epoch of rampant electrification, adds to the symbolic scenario. And then there is the meal, consisting of a pot-au-feu, a simple salad, and cider. "'This time it's a success!' exclaimed his wife, while serving each person a bouillon the color of mahogany, its surface a moiré of bronze waves, bubbling with topaz eyes. It was succulent and unctuous, robust and yet delicate, refined as it was by the addition of boiled chicken innards. Everybody was now silent, their noses in their plates, their faces kindled by fumigations from the aromatic soup."[15]

This welcoming dish immediately becomes the pretext for a vicious critique of restaurant culture by Durtel, one of the guests, who describes a restaurant in Paris where he dines once a month, certain that this establishment is guilty of poisoning its clients:

> While nibbling at the sauce au gratin of a redoubtable sole, I observed the customers who surrounded me, and I found them singularly changed since my last visit. They had either lost weight or were bloated; their eyes were either hollow and ringed with violet or sagging under double rose pouches; the fat people had turned yellow; the skinny ones green. . . . This interested me, as you can well imagine, and I turned myself into a course in toxicology and discovered, by studying myself while eating, the frightful ingredients that masked the taste of disinfected fish as well as of cadavers, powdery mixtures of carbon and tan, meats disguised by marinades and painted with sauces the color of sewers, wines colored with fuchsine, perfumed with furfurol, and thickened with molasses and plaster.[16]

Soon afterward, the evocation of blasphemy permits what had begun as a moralizing contrast between the natural and the artificial, the rural and the urban, to devolve into a discussion of the ultimate opposition between the sacred and the diabolic. In the context of his research on Gilles de Rais, the protagonist of the novel, des Hermies, offers a brief genealogy of satanism in France, specifically mentioning certain black masses of the seventeenth century celebrated by the Abbot Guibourg on the nude bodies of women, masses in which such notables of the royal court as Madame de Montespan were said to have participated.

> The ritual of these ceremonies was quite atrocious; generally, a child was carried off, and then burned in an oven in the countryside; then the remaining powder was mixed with the blood of another child whose throat had been slashed, so as to obtain a paste resembling that used by the Manicheans I told you about. The Abbot Guibourg officiated, consecrating the host by cutting it up into little pieces and mixing it with this blood darkened by ash; such was the matter of the Holy Sacrament.[17]

To add to this horror—where desecration is predicated upon the death of innocents; and where the sacred host, which should never even touch the teeth for fear of injury, is sliced up with a knife—is yet another form of Black Mass, the Mass of Sperm. The transubstantiation of the host is abjected by its satanic simulacrum; the spiritual life-giving host is replaced by the visceral marks of a sinful eroticism and an unholy death.

In this context, the symbolic articulation of *Là-bas* places tremendous allegorical importance on the pot-au-feu, as the culinary point of sanity and purity in an increasingly decadent world.[18] Indeed, the last chapter of the book begins with another meal in the belltower, where Madame Carhaix offers her guests the bouillon of the pot-au-feu that was made the night before. This bouillon, served with noodles, is at the center of the meal, accompanied by a salad of cold meat mixed with sour herring and celery root, a purée of potatoes and cheese, and dessert, all washed down with fresh cider. Durtal and des Hermies exclaim that her cooking is an incitement to the sin of gluttony, yet this joke is but an ironic prefiguration of yet another gastronomic metaphor, with which the novel concludes, expressing the full force of Huysmans's pessimism and antimodernism: "[T]his century doesn't give a damn about Christ in Glory; it contaminates the supernatural and vomits it out. How then can we have hope for the future, how can we imagine that the children born of those fetid bourgeois in these filthy times will be clean? Brought up in that way, I wonder what they will accomplish in life." Durtal replies: "They will do like their fathers, like their mothers. They will stuff their bellies and they will empty out their souls through their guts!"[19] This excremental vision, couched in the vilest of alimentary terms, is all the more forceful for the divine pot-au-feu which they are already digesting as they speak.

The symbolic destiny of the pot-au-feu takes a lighter, and certainly less conservative, turn in Marcel Rouff's beloved novel, *La vie et la passion de Dodin-Bouffant, Gourmet* (The Life and Passion of Dodin-Bouffant, Gourmet, 1924), a book dedicated to the memory, and friendship, of several great gastronomes, both living and dead: Brillat-Savarin, Curnonsky, Gabion, Guy de Pourtalès. In this tale of two meals, the protagonist, the great gourmet Dodin-Bouffant, is invited to a dinner hosted by the Prince of Eurasia (his name itself indicating the alien threats to French culinary integrity and perfection), who wishes to astonish his guests with a most perfect and extravagant meal. In a pastiche of the nineteenth-century French haute cuisine brought to its apogée by Carême, this feast, served in the already outmoded manner of the *service à la française* (several courses, each composed of many dishes presented simultaneously), is a veritable compendium of the sort of cooking codified by Escoffier at the turn of the century, and valorized by all so many twentieth-century chefs.[20]

First Course

**Soups:**

*Bisque de pigeon*

*Bisque de cailles au coulis à la reine*

*Bisque d'écrevisses*

*Bisque de soles farcies*

**Center Dish:**

*Marcassin*

**End Dishes:**

*Pâté royal*

*Terrine de faisans aux truffes vertes*

**Hors-d'oeuvres:**

*Perdreaux aux fines herbes à la broche, avec une essence de jambon*

*Poupetin de tourterelles*

*Saucissons à la dauphine*

*Brochet fourré*

**Large Main Dishes:**

*Poulardes farcies à la crème*

*Lapereaux à la Saingaraz*

*Oiseaux de rivière accommodés aux huîtres*

Wines: Dry Sherry after the soups; whites: Carbonnieux, Langon, Meursault, Pouilly; reds: La Chaînette, Thorins, Saint-Estèphe; between the first and second courses, Malvasia from Cyprus and Madeira.

Second Course

**Fish:**

*Lottes du lac de Genève à la vestale*

*Truites de torrent à la Chartreuse*

**Large Roasts:**

*Dindons à la daube*

*Côtes de boeuf à la hollandaise*

*Poitrine de veau au pontif, escortée de ris de veau et de quenelles*

*Gigot de mouton en filets farcis*

**Sauces:**

*Piquante*

*Au pauvre homme*

*Au bleu celeste*

*À la nichon*

**Salads:**

*D'herbes*

*D'oranges*

*D'olives*

**Side Dishes:**

*Chanterelles farcies*

*Crêtes en pagode au vin de Champagne*

*Asperges*

*Rôties en rocher*

*Laitances de carpes à la Béchamel*

*Truffes à la Maréchale*

Wines: whites: Haut-Preignac, Muscat de Frontignan, Jurançon, Seyssel; reds: Côte-Saint-Jacques, Cortaillod-en-Neuchâtel, Richebourg, Romanée-Conti; between the second and third courses: Tokay, grenache, Lacryma-christi, and sorbets au marasquin.

Third Course

**Soups:**

*Panade de blancs de poulardes*

*Bouillon de métonnage*

*Ouille au bain-marie*

**Main Dishes:**

*Hure de saumon*

*Lapins au Père Douillet*

*Oie à la carmagnole*

*Alouettes au gratin*

*Faisan en gondole*

*Terrine de bécasses*

**Hors-d'oeuvres:**

*Andouilles de poisson*

*Beignets de blanc-manger*

*Foie gras à la cendre*

**Desserts:**

*Compote de coings en gelée vermeille*

*Compote grillée de pêches*

*Pâtes d'avelines*
*Marmelade de violettes*
*Oranges douces et des poires à l'eau-de-vie*
*Candis de cannelle et de jonquille*
*Gaufres au vin d'Espagne*
*Cornets et des gimblettes*
*Massepains en laqs d'amour*
*Macarons au liquide*
*Glaces de rose, d'épine-vinette et de grenade*
*Ouvrages d'amande*
*Fromages glacés*
*Eaux de fenouil, de pistache, et d'orgeat*

Wines: whites: Yvorne, Rochecorbon, Puy-Notre-Dame, Vouvray; reds: Chambertin, Mouton-Lafite, Hermitage, Lunel; red Champagnes of Bouzy and Verzeney, and Port; followed by coffee, ratafias, blancs d'abricots de Grenoble, muscat, anis.

In his brilliant analysis of this book, "Savory Writing," Lawrence Schehr shows how this menu, rather than being part of the culinary narrative, exists as a rupture in the text due to its very excess, since it intentionally and necessarily surpasses the reader's culinary knowledge and imagination. One might well imagine reading this menu against several cookbooks and culinary encyclopedias, in order to decipher the often mysterious names, but this would already be to read the menu outside the confines of the fictional narrative. Indeed, even with the aid of the nearly 3,000 recipes offered in Escoffier's *Le Guide culinaire* (1903) or the approximately 7,000 recipes published in Gringoire and Saulnier's encyclopedic *Le Répertoire de la cuisine* (1914), the prince's menu would still remain partially opaque. Schehr explains the problem as follows:

> The prince's menu then is not only problematic because of the culinary sins, it is also difficult, unreadable, and indigestible, because of its gastronomic excess. If food is to be translated into discourse it must be manageable, easily ab-

> sorbed by the eye or the mouth, so that the coenaesthetic and synaesthetic effects, that is to say, the general bodily effects and the effects of the senses paired together, are developed in tandem. For gastronomy to work as a discourse within a literary work, there must be the possibility of an ekphrastic moment, be it either a description or a recipe.[21]

It is now Dodin-Bouffant's turn. For Rouff, the antithesis of this failure is a moment of culinary genius composed of the hyperbolically precise description of a hyperbolically perfect, and complex, dish. Needless to say, his estimation of the prince's meal is best summed up by the menu he had his cook, Adèle Pidou, create in reciprocation for and contradistinction to the prince's gargantuan and rather ridiculous effort. Against that vast compendium he sets a short menu, dramatically centered on a single dish. This meal, presented in the modern *service à la russe* (where one dish follows another), speaks for itself, especially given its centerpiece, which at this point can be easily intuited by the reader:

*Friandises avant le potage*
*Potage Adèle Pidou*
*Fritures de Brillat-Savarin*
*Pot-au-feu Dodin-Bouffant, paré de ses légumes*
*Purée Soubise*
*Desserts*
Wines: whites: Coteaux de Dézaley, Château-Grillé; reds: Châteauneuf-du-Pape, Ségur, Chambolle.[22]

That was all. Though his guests awaited with trepidation the pot-au-feu, that "gross lackey's dish,"[23] the triumph was total. And as a result, in a wonderful and unmoralistic celebration of mixed passions, Dodin-Bouffant fell in love with, and ultimately married, his cook. The description of the pot-au-feu is a masterpiece of culinary literature:

> The pot-au-feu itself, lightly rubbed with saltpeter and dusted with salt, was cut into slices, and was so fine that the mouth sensed, ahead of time, how deliciously breakable and crumbly this flesh would be. The aroma that emanated from it derived not only from the juices of the beef that steamed forth like incense, but also from the energetic odor of the tarragon with which it was impregnated, and from a very few cubes of transparent, immaculate lard which had been inserted into the meat. The rather thick slices of meat, whose velvetiness was already felt by the lips, rested gently upon a pillow composed of a large slice of sausage chopped up into pieces, the pork being accompanied by the finer flesh of veal, to which was added chopped thyme and chervil. Yet these delicate meats, cooked in the same bouillon as the beef, were themselves supported by an ample carving of chicken wings and breasts, boiled in their broth along with a veal knuckle, rubbed with mint and wild thyme. And to prop up this triple and magic superposition, the fat and robust support of a comfortable layer of fresh foie gras cooked simply in Chambertin had been audaciously slipped behind the white meat of the chicken, which had been fed solely with milk-soaked bread. The alternating disposition of ingredients followed the same order, forming layers clearly demarcated by an envelopment of assorted vegetables cooked in the bouillon and finished in butter.[24]

The exaltation of the guests was absolute, and this "simple, short, bourgeois"[25] meal was a far greater success than that of the prince. Dodin-Bouffant matched the overly complex menu of the prince with a tremendously—but, in the context of the narrative, not overly—complex recipe. Hyperbole contra hyperbole. Though this was undoubtedly a superb dish, today it would seem as overbearingly pompous and heavy (or even moreso) as many of those served by the Prince of Eurasia. In fact, this pot-au-feu is a masterpiece of haute cuisine presented, for moral, psychological, and narrative reasons, in the guise of a popular dish. It is clearly not the pot-au-feu that was to be had, more than a half-century later, at Léon de Lyon, nor that which is served in thousands of homes every day in France. It remains, however, a highly charged symbolic substitute imbued with domestic love, one whose complexity and perfection in no way detracts from its folkloric nature. Once again, the French earth has the upper hand over a soulless, decadent, suspiciously internationalized cuisine. However, Rouff—in his simultaneous celebration of literary, erotic, and culinary pleasures—was opposed to all moralizing (religious, social, medical, and otherwise). His pot-au-feu therefore transcends the regionalism that is the conservative underpinning of so much French politics and cooking. Dodin-Bouffant's pot-au-feu had to be out-of-the-ordinary, spectacular, a perfect synthesis of techniques and ingredients, otherwise it would be susceptible of falling into the same symbolic mold as so many other pot-au-feu of his epoch. This is what makes his dish both transcendent and transcendental.

As indicated by the dedication of his book, Marcel Rouff was friends with the most celebrated gastronome of his time, Curnonsky (the pseudonyme of Maurice Sailland—coincidentally, like that other great gastronome, Colette, a ghost-writer for Willy), "The Prince of Gourmets." Together, they helped establish and popularize the contemporary discourse of regional French cuisine. While the nineteenth century saw several efforts to establish such regional cuisines in Paris, they met with relatively little success. One of the most notable examples was that of the excellent restaurant Les Frères Provençaux, which soon had to transform its Provençal cuisine into a more Parisian model, due to a general lack of interest in the brothers' culinary origins. The regionalization of French cuisine had to await not only a reaction against the geographically limited ideals of the Parisian bourgeoisie, but also the advent of a more material phenomenon, the automobile. The first *Guide Michelin* published in the year 1900—created to facilitate travel by car (and thus to increase the use of tires, Michelin's major product)—was to have an inestimable effect on the history of French cuisine. As automobiles became increasingly comfortable, reliable, and fast, the concentric circles around Paris of touristic discovery, culinary and otherwise, rapidly increased. This investigation and celebration of the provinces served not only aesthetic purposes: the culinary symbolism of the French earth was already being placed in the service of a conservative, indeed reactionary, politics, where even the seeming innocence of Dodin-Bouffant might take on sinister implications in light of the global catastrophies to follow.

In 1919, Marthe Daudet—wife of Léon Daudet, editor of the reactionary journal *L'Action française*—published in Paris, under the pseudonyme Pampille, *Les bons plats de France,* a nostalgic gastronomic incarnation of political and religious conservatism. This antimodernist cookbook, a celebration of family values and peasant mores, of rural national cuisine and regional specialties, begins by demarcating the major regions of France by its four great national soups: pot-au-feu, onion soup, leek and potato soup, cabbage soup.[26] Listed first among these foundational recipes, the humble pot-au-feu has the prime place of honor in this discourse. This conservative symbolization of the earth and its bounties, of roots, blood, and race, was, on the gastronomic level, a direct attack against the French haute cuisine of the great Parisian restaurants and international hotels, a culinary tradition deemed degenerate in its overrefinement and its distance from the true source of all cuisine, the earth. It should be noted, of course, that this folkloric idealization of country cooking was at that moment a primarily Parisian phenomenon, promulgated precisely by such sophisticated gastronomes as Curnonsky. The semiologist Eugenio Donato explains how, for example, in regard to the 1855 classification of the wines of the Médoc, such essentialization was established, with "the form of metropolitan rationalization being extended to the provincial earth, in the guise of the reflection of an order locked in the earth itself."[27] The same might well be said for cuisine, insofar as the age-old issue of Parisian centralization and dominance versus regional insularity and independence is also played out within gastronomic discourse. Ironically, on the culinary level, the notion that a given wine or dish "cannot travel" assures a certain isolation of the provinces, to remain ever safe from Parisian (and by extension, "international" or "cosmopolitan," that is, leftist and decadent) appropriation. Symbolic closure entails psychological security.

While the automobile permitted the creation of a circuit of culinary discovery that extended from Paris to the provinces, the inverse circuit, from the provinces to Paris, was established by another great technological invention of the century, the radio. In 1928, the gourmet establishment La Maison Corcellet, along with the publisher Flammarion and Radio-Paris, initiated a competition that invited listeners (who were mostly women), to submit their best recipes, thus creating a multiregional network of culinary informants. The very first prize awarded went to a Madame Paul Julien from Chantilly, for her *ballotine d'agneau Judic,* and the winning recipes were eventually collated in a volume dedicated to regional cuisine. As Alberto Capatti explains, "A major consequence was that female cooks, until then relegated to the second rank by male chefs, by culinographs and by masculine gastronomic clubs, finally had their revenge."[28] Both the geographic and the class circles were closed, and the sundry regional cuisines finally achieved their proper gastronomic status, one that would eventually permit certain female chefs, such as the famed Mères Lyonnaises, to win Michelin's highest honors. Ironically, a conservative sensibility within the culinary symbolic would help advance, however slightly, the professional status of women.

One might have thought that by passing from fiction to reality, Dodin-Bouffant's pot-au-feu would have finally clarified such gastronomic myths. But the context says everything. On 27 November 1954, the famed chef Alexandre Dumaine created a menu centered on this dish at his restaurant the Hôtel de la Côte d'Or in the village of Saulieu. The meal was savored by Curnonsky, along with the members of the Club des Cent, a group created in 1912 both to partake in the joys of French cooking and to defend French culinary traditions against the ever-encroaching menaces of foreign cuisines. The menu was nearly, but not quite, as simple and significative as that of Dodin-Bouffant:

*Le velouté de Geline*
*Le turban de Lavoret Cardinalisé*
[wine: Puligny Montrachet Clos de la Pucelle, 1945]
*Le pot-au-feu aux quatre services de Dodin-Bouffant*
[wine: Le Morgon "Le Py"]
*La Toque du Président Adolphe Clerc*[29]

The *pot-au-feu aux quatre services de Dodin-Bouffant*—which hardly resembles that of Adèle Pidou in Rouff's novel—was cooked as follows. The consommé is made with veal hocks and knuckles, oxtail and gelatinous beef chuck, a small packet of fresh pork rind, and seasonal vegetables, cooked for three and half hours; the consommé is then divided into four earthenware kettles, to which are added ham, steamed chicken, sausages *(judrus)*, rump steak *(aiguillette de boeuf à la ficelle)*, and vegetables.The services of the pot-au-feu are then ordered as follows:

*Le judrus aux truffes et pistaches avec pommes natures au beurre frais*
*Le jambon avec une sauce Soubise*
*Les poulardes à la vapeur avec une mousseline de foie d'oie*
*L'aiguillette de boeuf avec les légumes de pot-au-feu, auxquelles on a jointe quenelles truffées, coeurs de céleri, fonds d'artichaut.*

It should be noted that what is traditionally recognized as a pot-au-feu consists of just the last part of the fourth service: *L'aiguillette de boeuf avec les légumes de pot-au-feu* (rump steak with boiled vegetables). Furthermore, by serving the ham with an onion sauce *(Soubise),* he even condenses two of Dodin-Bouffant's courses into a single part of a single dish! Indeed, the staggering complexity of this service—where a single dish has been distended into an entire menu—seems to synthesize the sensibilities of both Dodin-Bouffant *and* the Prince of Eurasia! Though this recipe is not at all a direct imitation of the pot-au-feu described in Rouff's book, it is more than sufficiently extravagant to bear witness to the same sources of culinary inspiration, or decadence, as the case may be. The sardonic polarization of culinary styles at the core of Rouff's novel becomes, in a mere thirty years, anachronistic, as the continual simplification of culinary style (if not technique)—due to a combination of aesthetic, dietary, and economic reasons—has already revealed Alexandre Dumaine's pot-au-feu to be as ostentatious as Adèle Pidou's was astounding.

A recent poll indicated that 17 percent of the French believe that pork spareribs belong in a pot-au-feu.[30] But is this any more shocking than the idea of adding foie gras to a pot-au-feu!? What can this statistic possibly mean in a postmodern gastronomic context, where new dishes increasingly exist as multiregional and polycultural hybrids, and where culinary "authenticity" has become a function of an ever mobile and dissatisfied nostalgia, such that "tradition" itself is continually rehabilitated and recreated? Decadence or progress? Reaction or renaissance? These reflections can be allegorically framed between two dishes. Before enjoying the pot-au-feu at Léon de Lyon, Chantal Thomas had the bad luck of ordering a first course of a suspiciously pleonastic nature: *une huître en gelée* (oyster in aspic). The redundancy of jellies—the aspic and the oyster itself—was rather disquieting and undelectable. In a similar vein, another dish, glimpsed at a different restaurant, was equally disturbing: a *pot-au-feu en gelée* (pot-au-feu in aspic), a paradoxical, oxymoronic, cold-hot-pot. Today, almost any boiled mixture of foodstuffs is named a "pot-au-feu" (for example, the *"pot au feu de poisson,"* a very popular fish version). The universal applicability of the term has thus voided its specificity, such that its current use value now joins its literal meaning (a pot on a flame) as an empty, open signifier.

The pot-au-feu, like regional cuisine in general, has for some time been absorbed into the now limitless global network of an haute cuisine in constant flux and hybridization, a state of affairs that, at least in its successful moments, certainly operates to the benefit of cuisine. The pot-au-feu has thus been rescued from a sinister symbolic fate. Unfortunately, as recent political discourse has made evident, the earth—despite the best efforts of those few radical Nietzscheans and Slow Food advocates still trying to liberate it—is continually being annexed for the most hideous of motives and the most destructive of politics. If only the joys of cooking could be matched by an equally joyful and liberatory political wisdom.

# 3
# In the Devil's Kitchen

*The meaning that flows in the veins of this mystical meat, whose every jolt is a kind of world, and another sort of parturition, loses and devours itself through the burns of an erroneous nothingness.*
—Antonin Artaud, *Correspondance de la momie*

Alberto Capatti, in *Le goût du nouveau: Origines de la modernité alimentaire* (The Taste of the New: The Origins of Alimentary Modernity), argues that modern gustatory sensibility is intricately linked to bachelor gourmets, and cites as notable examples Grimod de la Reynière, Le Marquis de Cussy, Brillat-Savarin, and Maurice Sailland. This fact might well be considered in relation to the notion, developed by Michel Carrouges, of *machines célibataires,* bachelor machines, inspired by Marcel Duchamp's masterpiece, *La Mariée mise à nu par ces célibataires, même* (The Bride Stripped Bare By Her Bachelors, Even, also known as The Large Glass.) The definition of the bachelor machine most germane to the present topic is given by Carrouges: "A bachelor machine is a fantastic image that transforms love into a mechanics of death."[1] Indeed, where is this transformation more directly symbolized than in the mechanics of eating, following the variously erotic trajectory from mouth to urethra and anus!? Rather than accentuate the incommensurable nostalgic distance between death and desire exemplified in Romanticism (a distance already lessened in Symbolism), the ultramodernist bachelor machines conflate Eros and Thanatos, suppress nostalgia, collapse time and eternity, and confuse origin and telos, so as to inaugurate an epoch where reproductive mechanical, electric, and electronic technologies inform erotic mechanics. Such transformations describe the solipsistic circuit of an onanistic sexuality (incorporating all possible dualisms and perversions); a delirious metaphysics (conflating all possible ontological contradictions); a useless simulation (where every machine is essentially infernal); and a morbid functionalism (where time, solitude, and death exist synonymously and contemporaneously). It is perhaps within this delirious psychic matrix that the joys (and anxieties) of cooking and eating may find their most extreme expressions.[2]

Suetonius, in *The Twelve Caesars,* informs us that the ruling vices of the Roman Emperor Vitellius were gluttony and cruelty, in that order. Vitellius would snatch pieces of meat off the sacrificial altars and devour them in the sight of the very gods he plundered. He banqueted four times a day, and continually invited himself to private banquets at all hours, costing his hosts a ruinous minimum of 4,000 gold pieces per meal; in one feast, offered by his brother, 2,000 fish and 7,000 game birds were served; in another, Vitellius dedicated a huge dish to the Goddess Minerva, naming it *The Shield of Minerva the Protectress,* consisting of the rarest victuals: pike livers, pheasant and peacock brains, flamingo tongues, and lamprey milt, all collected from the distant corners of his vast empire. Yet sheer luxury, excess, and gluttony never constitute gastronomy. On the same order, the fact that Cleopatra dissolved, in her beverage, a pearl worth six million sesterces created a most costly show of conspicuous consumption, and established an eternal culinary myth—yet it did little to advance the quality of cuisine. In a reflection on the *exquisite* in cuisine, the great food writer M. F. K. Fisher decries this sort of culinary absurdity. Castigating those sorts of gourmands who would, out of sheer ostentation, serve entire platters of the tongues of birds who were first taught to speak, she describes what would be a truly exquisite gesture: "But what if one of those epicures, greatly in love with a proud lady named Livia, had taught a thousand birds to sing her name, Livia, Livia, to the moment of most perfect diction, and then had served forth to the lady a fine pie of their tongues, split, honeyed, and impaled on twigs of myrrh?"[3] Beyond a certain threshhold, the vulgar becomes sublime—but what has this to do with gastronomy? The inverse is no less disturbing. What does it mean to claim, as did Grimod de la Reynière, in his *Itinéraire nutritif ou Promenade d'un gourmand dans divers quartiers de Paris* (Nutritive Itinerary, or the Promenade of a Gourmet in Diverse Neighborhoods of Paris), that "[t]he mustards of Maille are better known in the North than the verse of Racine"?[4]

Consider what is perhaps the most extreme, indeed apocalyptic, example of incorporation. The patient is beset by delusions of ruin and guilt. As a foreigner, now totally impoverished, he reproaches himself for not having taken out French citizenship, fearing this to be a serious crime. He anticipates a terrible punishment: a nail will be hammered into his head, and filth poured into his stomach; then he and the members of his family will be tortured, dismembered, and left exposed in a barren field. Finally, terribly mutilated, he will be led in a large procession to a fair and will be condemned to live until his death as a horrendous attraction in a cage with wild beasts.

> Accompanying these delusions of ruin, guilt, imminent punishment and persecution are interpretations of truly surprising extension. It is the "refuse policy," as he calls it, a policy which has been instituted especially for him. All the refuse, all the waste of the whole universe, is put aside for the purpose of being put into his stomach at some time. Everything is saved without exception. When someone smokes, there will be the ashes, the burnt match, and the

> cigarette stub. At meals he is preoccupied with crumbs, fruit pits, chicken bones, the water or wine that is left at the bottom of the glass. He says the egg is his worst enemy because of the shell; it is also the expression of the great anger of his persecutors. When someone sews, there are bits of thread and needles. All the matches, strings, bits of paper, and glass that he sees while walking in the street are meant for him. Then come nail parings, hair clippings, empty bottles, letters and envelopes, subway tickets, newspaper wrappings, dust brought in on people's shoes, bath water, kitchen garbage from all the restaurants in France, etc. Then it is rotten fruits and vegetables, cadavers of men and animals, the urine and feces of horses. When you talk about a clock, he says you are speaking of the hands, cogs, springs, case, weight, key, etc., all of which he will have to swallow. These interpretations bear on everything, absolutely everything, that he sees or imagines.[5]

This excessive and disquieting case study, dating from 1923, of a patient suffering from depressive psychosis is the antithesis of Kafka's hunger artist. Here—where the surreal devolves into the Kafkaesque, which in turn degenerates into the Ubuesque—it is as if, in a fit of paranoid megalomania, man the microcosm opened his mouth to reveal, in simultaneous punishment and revenge against the cosmos, an infinite black hole that would devour the macrocosm which he was to become. For what phantasm can be more primal than to devour the cosmos, like Zeus, or to devour oneself? What image is more poetic than an eater of stars? The imagination—be it quotidian, poetic, pathological—is but the ephemera of partial objects torn from culture and history, the transgression by fragmentation of a contemporary cosmos all too unified and all too controlled to admit the most singular, and idiosyncratic, phantasms of our desires. Food constitutes, par excellence, such assimilable, partial objects, such expendable objects of desire.

Such cosmic polymorphous perversity was expressed in a very different light by Jean Genet in *Notre-Dame-des-Fleurs* (1948):

> It happened one morning morning that I placed my lips with an objectless love on the frozen handrail of the Rue Berthe, and another time I kissed my own hand, and yet another time, worn out by emotion, I wanted to swallow myself by turning my boundlessly open mouth inside out over my head, letting my entire body, and then the Universe, enter, no longer being anything but a ball of eaten substance that would be annihiliated little by little: this is my way of seeing the end of the world.[6]

The world, as well as death, is most immediately experienced through ingestion, in both the literal and figurative senses of the word. In *Pompes funèbres* (1953), Genet literalizes that incorporation which is an integral part of the work of mourning. Bemoaning the death of his lover, the narrator fantasizes:

> Since it was impossible that I bury him all by myself in an intimate ceremony (I could have taken his body, and why wouldn't the powers-that-be permit it?, cut it up into pieces in a kitchen and eaten them. Many scraps would certainly remain: the intestines, the liver, the lungs, and especially the eyes with their lids bordered by lashes, which I would have dried and burned, keeping the ashes to mix with my food, so that the flesh could be assimilated with my own), let him therefore depart with those official honors whose glory will rebound upon myself and slightly stifle my despair.[7]

The most extreme erotic fantasies, of cannibalism and necrophilia, serve as both the expression of an infinite tenderness and as a critique of the murderous history of political culture.

The Roman Emperor Heliogabalus once sent hunters to the land of Lydia, offering two hundred pieces of gold to the man who brought back a phoenix. None did. It is difficult to gauge the meaning of this gesture by the man whom Antonin Artaud characterized as the "crowned anarchist," who, perhaps tired of the repeated human sacrifices to his own divine nature, sought a rarer offering. For Heliogabalus, true to his own solar name, wished to bring heaven down to earth, in a cruel and erotic scenario of death. The blood of the sacrifices organized by the Priest of the Cult of the Sun, flowing from the sacrificial altars of the Temple of Emesa, must not be allowed to course through normal sewers to the sea. Rather, a special system was necessary, as Antonin Artaud described in *Héliogabale ou l'anarchiste couronné* (Heliogabalus or the Anarchist Crowned, 1934): "Through these sewers—in the form of an ardent tendril, whose circumference diminished as they reached into the depths of the earth—the blood of beings sacrificed in prescribed rites would regain the sacred corners of the earth, touching primitive geological veins, with congealed shudderings of chaos."[8] Such blood—ambivalent symbol of life and death—is food for the gods.

Sacrifice is a form of communication, and a primal condition for community; it is a manner of resolving the enigmas of existence and illuminating the mysteries of our origins. Sacrifice mediates the contradictions inherent in the polarizations between life and death, heaven and hell, past and future, time and eternity, creation and apocalypse, body and spirit, host and guest. Within a theological system, the symbolic is inaugurated by the violence of sacrifice, which transforms the body into a signifier, bound to circulate within a restricted economy of exchange. The sacred implies mystery, or mystification. When the internal contradictions of this mystery principle demand resolution, it is manifested in sacrilege as an attempt to transcend both the limits of individuality and the boundary between sacred and profane. Such wisdom is thus a function of blasphemy, abomination, and transgression. Whence the double significance of Heliogabalus's quest: sacred sacrifice, profane cuisine. The phoenix would be the mythological, culinary emblem or equivalent of the Rite of the Sun. The Phoenix has a quite definite, indeed overdetermined, history. Its cycle is described by Jean-Pierre Vernant:

> The incandescent life of the Phoenix follows a circular course, increasing and decreasing, with birth, death and rebirth following a cycle that passes from an aromatic bird closer to the sun than the eagle flying at great heights, to the state of a worm in rotting matter, more chthonian than the snake or the bat. From the bird's ashes, consumed at the end of its long existence in a blazing aromatic nest, is born a small earth-worm, nourished by humidity, which shall in turn become a phoenix.[9]

This creature has a life cycle that is the very allegory of myth itself; it is also, not coincidentally, an allegory of cuisine, taken in its structural instance, as it spans the antithetical conditions of: raw / cooked, cold / hot, fresh / rotten, moist / dry, gamy / aromatized. The phoenix would thus be the perfect dish and the ideal offering, paradoxically encompassing the contradictory possibilities of diverse cooking techniques, inherent alimentary difference, and sacred symbolism. Like the transubstantiation of the host, or cannibalistic communion, the eating of the phoenix would constitute a truly transcendental gastronomic act.

The aesthetics of intoxication finds its demonic inversion in the work of Antonin Artaud, whose life instantiates the ultimate implosion and destruction of the sublime. Where Baudelaire sought an artificial paradise, Artaud found an artificial hell, for flesh has rarely been so tormented, a soul rarely so bewitched, a voice so threatened. The soul is something of the body; God is the manifestation of organic secretions; grammatical reflexivity returns speech to its corporeal origins; thought is shaken to its core by a foreign volition, by "sudden and unforeseen electricity."[10] For Artaud, "the liver is the filter of the unconscious, while the spleen is the physical guarantor of the infinite."[11] Addicted to opiates early in life, Artaud's liver and spleen were saturated with intoxicants even moreso than his spirit was entranced by Baudelaire. His unconscious was skewed, infinity foreshortened, nerves frayed; his core was sometimes felt as an amorphous or fragmented mass, sometimes as nothingness itself. Only by overcoming the difference between force and form—the very antinomy at the base of metaphysics—can the essence of life be grasped, one equal to the "fragile and fluctuating core untouched by forms" that he sensed at the center of his existence.[12] Wishing to regain a long-lost primal unity, he sought a cure to his pain and his emptiness through a lifelong use of intoxicants, magic, and arcana. Indeed, a lifetime of opiates (and their moralistic pharmacological inversion, bismuth cures) hardly sufficed to reduce his torments; a certain metaphysical homeopathy was necessary. The paroxystic theater of cruelty announced in *Le théâtre et son double* (The Theater and Its Double) was defined as a sort of curative magic, intended to touch the marrow, eliminating the differences between theater and world, art and life; as such, the theater would become a mythopoeic stage, and the world would be a theater.

The articulatory moment between theater and madness, poetry and delirium, occurred during his trip in 1936 to Mexico, at which point theater and hallucination, cosmology and psychology, all began to merge. Artaud had long been obsessed by the idea of Mexico, a Baroque Mexico, volcanic earth, Indian blood, magical realities, chimerical visions, a culture of fire, of the sun: an ancient solar culture founded on the supremacy of death, where destruction is a precondition of rebirth and transformation.[13] There, everything is already hieratic, already cruel, as in the theater of which he dreamed. Such is the immemorial Indian culture that burns organisms, boils the blood, irrigates the nerves: "The civilization of Mexico lives on a nightmare of organs,"[14] writes Artaud, echoing "the limbo of a nightmare of bones and muscles" with which he had long before characterized his own existence in *Fragments d'un journal d'enfer* (Fragments of a Journal from Hell).[15] Artaud's Mexico was bound by the preconceptions and idiosyncratic symbols of his own partially ecstatic, partially pathological, partially visionary phantasms. After his return to Paris and his descent into madness, the culture of the Tarahumaras would inform first his psychotic delirium, and later his transformation of poetry. This inner Mexico was a fertile nervous illumination or stimulation, strangely resembling Artaud's impossible theater of cruelty. It was in the land of the Tarahumaras that Artaud discovered, and was bewitched by, a scenario that coincided with his desires: the rite of Tutuguri. To reach this land, Artaud—having discarded the last of his opiates, thus being without narcotics for the first time in seventeen years—traversed a forest of signs, bewitched. Alongside every road sprouted a burnt tree in the form of a cross, signs that he was approaching his goal. The mountains revealed hallucinated figures of men tortured by gods, amongst which nature capriciously disclosed the image of a nude man nailed to the rocks and tortured under a volatilized sun: Artaud crucified at Golgotha.[16] To reach the land of the Tarahumaras, Artaud experienced twenty-eight days of arduous and hallucinatory journey, symptoms of drug withdrawal, psychic turbulence, vast expectations: he was reduced to "a heap of poorly assembled organs."[17]

His trajectory led him through a Tarahumara village dominated by giant decorated phalli, which could not but have caused him to recollect his own tale of that other solar God, Heliogabalus, and of the colossal ten-ton stone phallus that preceded this emperor's triumphal march into Rome.[18] The sun is the most generalized manifestation of energy, of force contra form, a sign of infinity, of eternity, of God. Artaud would write in *Héliogabale* of this Emperor-God, "son of the summits, false Antonin, Sardanapalus, and finally Heliogabalus, a name that seems to be the auspicious grammatical contraction of the highest denominations of the sun."[19] Antonin Artaud would inscribe his own name in this solar theology, celebrating the "false Antonin" as a Sun God who is the very principle of anarchy, the breath of chaos itself, a breath that would pierce the body and excite the nerves. Artaud participated in the Rite of Ciguri, the Rite of Tutuguri, led by the Priests of the Sun acting as manifestations of the Word of God. Ciguri isn't simply peyote, but rather the god himself who enters one's nerves; *Ciguri consequently entails the very incorporation of infinity.*[20] But for Artaud, the Tutuguri does not represent the "inner sun" of Baudelaire's artificial paradises; rather, it evokes the black sun of Nerval's despair: "Created for the external glory of the sun, *Tutuguri* is a black rite. The rite of the black night and of the *eternal* death of the sun. No, the sun shall no longer return . . . "[21] For Artaud, who will come to claim that "I am infinity," these events were a formative experience at the core of both his delirium at Rodez and the subsequent poetic reconstitution of his own body.[22]

The therapeutic action of this ritual depends on the total pillaging and purgation of the organism: Ciguri is man himself assassinated by God.[23] This devastating metaphysical homeopathy was to be desublimated by Artaud into an anticultural poetics, where the phantasmatic return to Mexico entailed the reconstitution of his previous inner turmoil and torment into a radically new poetics. His spleen was transformed into an immense emptiness, an oceanic void upon which a fire-sprouting root was stranded; this was the root of the peyote plant, the root of Ciguri, made one with self and world. As things returned to normal, Artaud didn't know whether it was he himself or the world that had fainted. Regardless, he had seen the spirit of Tutuguri.

Although, during the rite of the Ciguri, Artaud explains that "I was ready for all the burns, and I awaited the first-fruits of the fire, in view of a soon to be generalized combustion"[24]—

invoking the actor signaling through the flames that has become the icon of the theater of cruelty—he was hardly prepared for the other apocalypse that was to follow, during his years of incarceration in the psychiatric hospital of Rodez, the "artificial death" of electroshock. In a postscript to "Le rite du peyotl chez les Tarahumara" (The Tarahumaras Peyote Ritual) we are informed that he wrote "Le rite du peyotl" after having suffered years of systematic empoisonment and torture, and that this text was his first attempt to return to himself. The belief in empoisonment (both real and imaginary), typical to psychosis, took many forms, including the culinary. In *Ci-Gît* (Here Lies), one of Artaud's final works, a sort of living testament, he discloses one of the many nightmarish torments he suffered, likened to a "horrible plague" (already announced in the section of *Le théâtre et son double* entitled *Le théâtre et la peste* [The Theater and the Plague]):

> You didn't know this
> that the EGG
>                         state
> was the anti-
> Artaud state
> par excellence
> and that to poison Artaud
> there is nothing
> like whisking up
> a good omelette
> in the spaces
> aiming at the gelatinous
> point
> which Artaud
> seeking for the man to be made
> has fled
> like a horrible plague
> and it is this point

they put back in him,
nothing like a good poison
cyanide and capers stuffed omelette,
transmitted by the air to his cadaver
to disarticulate Artaud
in the anathema of his bones
HANGED ON THE INTERNAL CADASTRE.[25]

*Cadastre / cadavre:* according to Artaud, any attempt to chart his interior would be doomed to failure, as one would find nothing but an incommensurable void or an unpredicable infinity. This ontological antinomy is indeed symbolized and anthropomorphized by the antithesis of the egg as the "anti-Artaud state" and the "body without organs" (a sort of human egg) as the delirious utopia that manifests the final state of the theater of cruelty, announced in his last work, the radiophonic *Pour en finir avec le jugement de dieu* (To Have Done With the Judgment of God, 1948). Camille Dumoulié offers a repertory of possible interpretations of the body without organs: that unframed space in which human life perpetually escapes its "frame"; a new strategy of humor, imposing an ungraspable reality upon thought; a secular renewal of the gnostic ideal of the glorious body and the mystic notion of the resurrected body; the libidinal body anterior to the constitution of the imaginary; the body of pure desire; a totally literary creation, constituting the transferential body that links author and reader. He concludes, however: "So as to undo the concept, it is necessary to anticipate the concept in the gesture, the dance, of the body and the organs. There are no rules to do so; every body is master of the game, sworn to its singularity, alone capable of inventing its own lines of flight beyond the frames of subjectivity and the organism."[26] Perhaps, in this case, the egg—like the body without organs—however equivocal, is a symbol for Artaud alone. In any case, the body without organs manifests the ruin of synaesthesia and signifies the end of the ideal of the total work of art.

Needless to say, cuisine was never an aesthetic matter for

Artaud, but rather—especially given the horrendous wartime conditions he suffered in the several psychiatric hospitals where he was interned, deprivations that ravished his body and soul—it was a matter of survival. He made this quite clear in a letter written from Rodez: "Jabberwocky is the work of a coward who did not want to suffer his work before writing it, and that can be seen. It's the work of a man who ate well, and that can be felt in his writing. I like the poems of the starving, the sick, the outcast, the poisoned: François Villon, Charles Baudelaire, Edgar Poe, Gérard de Nerval . . ."[27] It is not by accident that these poets, who constitute Artaud's private poetic genealogy, form a pantheon of writers who both experienced and celebrated intoxications of various sorts. The antithesis of the egg state *and* the egg-like characteristics of the body without organs are in fact perfectly coherent with Artaud's schizoid metaphysics, ruled not by a syllogistic logic governed by the law of noncontradiction, but rather by an illogic organized according to the rhetorical structures of the inclusive disjunction. While for Minkowski's patient the "egg is his worst enemy," for Artaud the egg was both enemy *and* the only ideal that remained. As Gillen Deleuze and Félix Guattari explain in *Mille plateaux* (A Thousand Plateaux):

> Matter equals energy. Production of the real as intensive magnitude starting from zero. This is why we consider the body without organs as a full egg before the extension of the organism and the organization of the organs, before the formation of strata, the intense egg that is defined by axes and vectors, gradients and thresholds, dynamic tendencies with a mutation of energy, cinematic movements with displacements of groups, migrations, and all of this independant of *accessory forms,* since organs appear and function here only as pure intensities.[28]

The egg as poison; the egg as force field; the egg as utopia: Artaud's ultimate allegory would maintain the contradictions that haunted him, and inspired him, throughout his entire life. Only now he had finally filled the void.

"Le rite du peyotl" was written in a temporary state of religious conversion—which Artaud later saw as a form of bewitchment—after having swallowed between 150 and 200 hosts.[29] No longer a theological homeopathy, this eucharistic overdose was part of a Christological delirium, briefly syncretized with Tarahumaras theology. This conversion was not to last long, and he soon renounced the Catholic faith in a most violent and obscene manner, and began writing the series of last works that finally instantiated the theater of cruelty, a cruelty inscribed on his own body, expressed by his own soul, and nuanced by the sundry intoxications that affected the psychic tenor of his entire life—opium, laudanum, bismuth, peyote, eucharistic wafers, as well as that of electroshock therapy, the electric drug. The rite of Tutuguri was one more instance of such intoxication, the desire to overcome the metaphysical anguish and the existential antinomies that tormented Artaud: to replace the emptiness within his body by incorporating infinity, to transform his psychic and physical pain into theatrical forms, to speak from the point of view of the dead, to finally have done with the judgments of man and God.

In this delirious theology, this hallucinatory theater, the sublime is indistinguishable from the counter-sublime—the sublime is interiorized, entailing the confusion of the senses, the wreck of the body, the dissipation of thought. The modernist conceptual trajectory of the aesthetics of intoxication epitomized by Baudelaire ends with Artaud: the implosion of the sublime engenders an anti-aesthetic that transforms all culinary effects into poison, and all transcendental forms into pain. This destiny of the interiorization of infinity was predicated, in some small part, on both a catharsis caused by violent intoxication and the rejection of food as poison. Such is an extraordinary purification that offers a foundation upon which rests part of the aesthetics, though certainly not the practice, of the gastronomic arts.

# 4
# The Epic of the Cephalopod

> Who would pride oneself on a "complete" experience of love? Only a monster of multiplicity, an octopus-man endowed with as many tentacles as the innumerable desires that give an appearance of meaning and an illusion of necessity to our existence, and which, in their totality, constitute the great delusion of our lives.
>
> —Alberto Savinio, *Nuova Enciclopedia*

Consider the cephalopod represented in Victor Hugo's ink and wash drawing of an octopus, *Pieuvre* (c. 1866), a black, nearly formless stain that evokes the morbid, lugubrious aspect of this animal, described by Hugo: "One would say a beast made of ash that inhabits the water. It is spiderlike in form and chameleonlike in coloration."[1] As is the case for the most extreme examples of zoological and botanical classes, such animals touch on the limits of monstrosity, evoking worldly fears and unconscious anguish. One can, in fact, localize the source of the octopus as monster par excellence, as a creature of nightmares and terror, an icon of the horrors of death: it was the moment when Victor Hugo, in *Les travailleurs de la mer* (The Toilers of the Sea, 1866), substituted the local word *pieuvre,* used mainly in the Channel Islands, for the more common term *poulpe.* One should remember that in French, the word for the living animal is usually different from that of the carcass to be transformed into foodstuff; Hugo's differentiation between *poulpe* and *pieuvre* takes this transformative logic one step further, for while normally man eats *poulpe,* in *Les travailleurs de la mer* the opposite is true, as *pieuvre* threatens to eat man, in the most horrendous of manners.

This moment of inestimable horror occurs when the protagonist, Gilliatt, in the process of exploring a hidden grotto on the coast, is caught in the grip of a giant octopus. This animal is a monster, the very "enigma of evil," "a viscosity with a will," a boneless, bloodless, fleshless creature with a unique orifice equivocally and disquietingly serving as both mouth and anus. Endowed with eight powerful tentacles covered with hundreds of blood-sucking suction cups, the octopus borders on the chimerical—"a medusa served by eight snakes"—as if coming from a world other than our own. Its attack is pure terror:

> It is a pneumatic machine that attacks you. You are dealing with a footed void. Neither claw thrusts nor tooth bites, but an unspeakable scarification. A bite is formidable, but less so than such suction. The claw is nothing compared to the sucker. The claw, that's the beast that enters your flesh; the sucker, that's you yourself who enter into the beast. Your muscles swell, your fibers twist, your skin bursts beneath this unworldly force, your blood spurts and frightfully mixes with the mollusc's lymph. The beast is superimposed upon you by its thousand vile mouths; the hydra is incorporated in the man; the man is amalgamated with the hydra. The two make one. This dream is upon you. The tiger can only devour you; the octopus, what horror, breathes you in! It draws you toward itself and into itself, and, bound, stuck, powerless, you slowly feel yourself emptied out within that horrendous sack, that monster. Beyond the terror of being eaten alive is the ineffability of being drunk alive.[2]

Here, monstrosity gains a new dimension, the reduction of anatomy to an absolute orifice. This "indescribable horror" inexorably leads to the "horror of the indescribable," analyzed by Laurent Jenny in *La terreur et les signes* (Terror and Signs) in terms of the poetics of unfigurability to be found at the limits of a certain modernist literature, notably in Hugo, Roussel, Artaud. The octopus represents a zoological manifestation of the temptation of the void, the equivocation of the formless, the horror of ungraspable monstrosity.

> Hugo's octopus is not satisfied being merely the gravedigger of the living: the entire sensible world comes to be buried within it piece by piece, wayward residues with which its monstrosity is nourished. In the octopus, the natural orders are reconciled in an unsettling grip where the rag is protracted into glue, ash into flesh, and the fold of the wave into the mouth. Therefore, through a mystery symmetric with the divine, the octopus is both part of the world and an exit out of the world, both form and the site of the completion of forms. Here, divine radiation is produced otherwise. It escapes from internal weightiness. It is diffusion and not conjunction. Its plenitude is unimpaired by the virtuality of the differences it engenders.[3]

In fact, it is zoologically the case that the squid, and not the octopus, occasionally grows to giant proportions. Indeed, Linnaeus even included in the first edition of his *Systema Naturae* a species referred to as *Sepia microcosmos,* to describe the giant squid; by 1861 the first demonstrable evidence of giant cephalopods was offered; and such vast creatures —referred to as Kraken, Devil-fish, Blood-Suckers—continue to excite the popular imagination. Hugo describes the creative logic behind this perversion of creation:

> At certain moments, one would be tempted to think that the ineffable which floats in our dreams encounters, in the realm of the possible, magnets that attract its lineaments, and that beings emerge from these obscure fixations of the dream. The Unknown disposes of marvels, and it

> makes use of them to compose monsters. Orpheus, Homer and Hesiod only managed to make the Chimera; God made the Octopus. When God wishes, he excels in the execrable.[4]

While Hugo criticizes God for creating the octopus, masterpiece of fright, Lautréamont turns this terror against its own creator. In *Les chants de Maldoror,* he imagines a creature to torment God: "Maldoror changed into an octopus, moving against his body his eight monstrous arms, each solid lash of which could easily have embraced the circumference of a planet."[5] But it is perhaps Jules Michelet who best summed up, in *La Mer* (The Sea, 1861), the continual source of fascination, in the literal sense of the term, with such cephalopods: "You are more mask than being."[6]

In *La seiche* (The Squid, 1998), the autobiographical novel by Maryline Desbiolles, the shortest sentence may well overturn and transform certain commonplace myths about French cuisine, where Marcel Rouff's pot-au-feu and Roland Barthes's *steak-frites* have long reigned as signs of the essence of popular French cooking. This sentence is the holophrase, "Aillés."[7] "Garlicky": the word is revelatory of the author's gastronomic, sensual, and poetic sensibilities. It should be noted, for example, that when Pampille (Marthe Daudet) established her repertory of French cuisine in *Les Bons plats de France* by dividing up the country according to its great soups—*pot-au-feu, soupe à l'oignon, soupe aux choux, soupe aux poireaux et aux choux*—the existence of Provençal cuisine is completely suppressed.[8] No *soupe à l'ail,* no *soupe au pistou,* no *soupe de poisson,* no *bourride,* no *bouillabaisse*—nothing that indicates the presence of a cuisine to the south of the great French culinary watershed marked by the butter / olive oil line, or otherwise stated, the great garlic divide. In our times, when haute cuisine in France and the United States is deeply influenced by a Mediterraneanizing vogue, the mosiac or palimpsest that composes "French cuisine" is becoming denser and more complex. Indeed, many of the most interesting and innovative restaurants today are those that combine, in a single menu or even a single dish, butter and oil, the raw and the cooked, the high and the low, the familiar and the strange. The exotic may now come from both remote places or the immediate neighborhood, from past times or the present, from unexpected juxtapositions or unheard of techniques.

For Maryline Desbiolles, the recipe for stuffed squid—the stages of which divide the book into twelve chapters—reveals the difference between French cuisine and its Provençal other:

> 1. Clean the squid, being careful not to tear them; 2. put aside the head and the tentacles 3. then chop up 3 onions, 1 clove of garlic, bacon and parsley. 4. Sauté the chopped ingredients in 2 soup spoons of olive oil, add the uncooked rice (a full cup), salt and pepper. 5. Fill each squid 3/4 full with this stuffing 6. and sew up the openings with kitchen thread. 7. In a casserole, sauté 2 chopped onions in two spoons of oil 8. and add the stuffed squid, which were browned in a pan on the rest of the olive oil; 9. flame in cognac, 10. add white wine, garlic, a bouquet garni, parsley, tomato paste, salt and pepper, 11. slide in a bit of cayenne pepper (or 1 to 3 bird's-tongue pimentos, according to taste) 12. and let simmer for about 3/4 of an hour.[9]

This recipe articulates both the narrative and the symbolic structure of the book, all the while marking the variegated trajectory from reality to fiction through numerous digressions. The squid that the narrator saw as a child in the oceanographic museum in Monaco—the city where today one may enjoy the highest sublimation of the hybridization of Mediterranean and haute cuisine in Alain Ducasse's renowned restaurant Louis XV[10]—the seductive, petrifying squid, is made the symbol of both life and death. For this child, who emigrated from the mountains of Savoy to the back country of Nice, the simple experience of seeing a *pissaladière* (a Niçois onion tart) emerge from an oven was enough to make of that stove "the doors of the unknown."[11] For the adult author, the kitchen, and more precisely the recipe for stuffed squid, continues to offer the basis for a meditation about her predilection for exploring the unknown and its relations to her own origins and ends.

The narrator explains, at one point, "But for the moment I only want the squid for the fragility of its doubtful whiteness, for the subtleness of its white coat"[12]—an animal curiously whiter than milk, whiter than snow. The unknown has, by definition, no color; whence, for example, the intensity of the terror inspired by Moby Dick, whose whiteness was not just a color, but a metaphysical condition. This anguishing strangeness suggests the necessity of establishing an iconology of *La seiche,* a book traversed by a constant and troubling slippage from white to whitishness, from whiteness to whitening; a tale in which white is neither color nor light, but the very texture of existence, the interior fiber of desire and pain, the certain premonition of death. Given my own family name, *Weiss*—whiteness in its pure, abstract state; a strange and foreign whiteness; a disquieting name for a writer—I cannot be indifferent to the figural play derived from the author's name, *Desbiolles,* equally linked (not directly, but through a botanical intermediary) to the color white: "But I was even furthermore convinced that whiteness was not as dreary as I had thought when I learned that my name, that of my father, came from the birch tree, whose silver-white bark made it the most attractive of all trees."[13] And this name, this onomastic whiteness, was also inscribed in her culinary destiny, signified by rice, that "delicate and nacreous hyphen"[14] connecting her family's Italian origins and her own birth in Savoy. This emigration was marked by the passage from her grandmother's *risotto* to *riz à la béchamel,* a rice and a sauce that could not but evoke the horizon of her childhood, the "eternal snow above the fir trees."[15] This whiteness triumphed once again in the squid, symbol of the strangeness that the Midi, the South of France, would always remain for her. Squid, garlic, rice (with grains "more diaphanous than pearly"), onions (obviously the white and not the yellow ones), white wine, salt ("use the saltshaker without temperence")—this dish bears all the psychological value of the white sheet under which the author, as a child, imagined, "milky waters from which emerged an entire world, terrifying and feverish."[16]

In this idiosyncratic cosmography, the color white is used as a veritable symbol of a universe. But despite the monochromatic aspect of this creative matrix, the squid symbolizes a complex existence: "It was really in the nature of this animal, with its changing name and fluctuating morphology, to plunge us into confusion from the very beginning."[17] Milky, murky waters have always inspired writers and artists, whence the duality of the iconography of *La seiche,* alternating between a chromatic (or rather achromatic) exemplification of whiteness and a mysterious zoological (and teratological) iconography. The story commences with the sentence: "The recipe begins with an error,"[18] indicating a mistake, or an ambiguity, of nomination. For the squid (*seiche*) exists in a confusion of names: *calmar, calamar, encornet, tautenne, suppion, scipion,* "and its clique, the devil-fish *(pieuvre),* the octopus *(poulpe),* and other medusae." This animal's fluctuating, indeed formless, morphology and equivocal nomination provide it with an equally volatile iconology, as well as with its own specific genealogy.

For Desbiolles, the domains of Eros and Thanatos symbolized by the squid are simultaneously multiplied and dissimulated in the depths of the narrator's body, as the very conditions of her femininity. Life is manifested by a dirty white monstrosity, "that vile egg which was obscene, and not the orangishness of my ovaries."[19] And there is also the egg of death—the sign of the pain of the nearly mortal accident she suffered—"a large egg navigating in my body."[20] As an infant, the narrator fell into a basin of boiling water, and was totally scalded over nearly her entire body, except, in mythical fashion, for her feet and ankles. In this amnesia-producing shock—which left her grandmother, who felt responsible for the tragedy, aphasic for months; and which was kept under a veil of silence in her family—the future cook was herself cooked. By beginning the paragraph that introduces this tragedy, "The stuffing *[farce]* is still steaming and burning hot,"[21] the tragedy is ironically defined as a "farce" (both comedy and stuffing), linking it to the future culinary passion and symbolism; the writing of the book entails a double catharsis, of past tragedy and future mortality. The imagery of the "Death and the Maiden" theme is henceforth enriched, and gastronomy is, quite exceptionally, related to death itself. (It is true that in the *Physiologie du goût,* Brillat-Savarin, while enumerating the many uses of sugar, reminds us that it can also be useful in the art of embalming, though this fact remains of little consequence for the history of cuisine.)[22]

The psychic source of this cephalopodic symbol of death is expressed, in all its terror, by Artaud in "Correspondance de la momie" (The Mummy's Correspondence, 1927), a meditation on the question of suicide: "But this death is much more refined; this death multiplied by myself exists through a sort of rarefaction of my flesh. The intelligence has no more blood. The squid of nightmares spurts all its ink to obstruct the outlets of the spirit; it is blood emptied from the veins, meat oblivious to the cut of the knife."[23] While Artaud never conquered the inner squid of his torments, Hugo's protagonist, Gilliat, vanquished the giant octopus: "Gilliat plunged the point of his knife into the flat viscosity and, with a gyrating movement like the twist of a whiplash, making a circle around the two eyes, ripped off the head like one pulls out a tooth. It was over. The entire beast fell. It resembled a fallen piece of laundry. The sucking pump destroyed, the void was undone."[24] As for Desbiolles, her accurate knifework—taking care *not* to tear the beasts's flesh—assured the success of the dish, though the squid took its revenge otherwise, in a more purely psychological manner.

The narrative of *La seiche* is polymorphous, vacillating between childhood and adulthood, life and death, Eros and Thanatos, macrocosm and microcosm, gastronomy and psychology: when we reach the point of the recipe where the narrator explains that, "now we must stuff the phantom,"[25] the squid has already taken on an excessive and incommensurable symbolism. A dish is a symbol; inspiration comes from aromas, tastes, techniques; but meaning derives from elsewhere, from a place most often unnameable and unattainable. In *La seiche,* the ambivalent phantom—squid, self, Death—is variously founded on a confusion of names, a rich polychromaticism paradoxically exisiting within the confines of whiteness, and a narrative enriched by subtle allusions and complex correspondences: the narrator could indeed claim that, *"La seiche, c'est moi."* For each and every sentence of this book—written to counter the "freeze-dried words"[26] all too often pronounced by her dinner guests—makes of cuisine an allegory of writing itself. What more appropriate definition of fiction, in a post-Nietzschean world, than, "a lie to create beauty"?[27] Whence the necessity of the fiction-inspiring error in the recipe with which the book began. However, this goes beyond the allegorical, since for Desbiolles—for whom cuisine "offers the words of my memory"[28]—the relation between cuisine and literature is certainly akin to the source of inspiration of that most illustrious drinker, François Rabelais, who wrote in the prologue of *Le Tiers livre* (The Third Book, 1546), "Icy beuvant je délibère, je discours, je résoulz et concluds. Après l'épilogue je riz, j'escriptz, je compose, je boy. Ennius beuvant escrivoit, escrivant beuvoit" ("While drinking I deliberate, I discourse, I resolve and conclude. After the epilogue I laugh, I write, I compose, I drink. Anxious, I write drinking, and drink writing").[29] *In vino* not *veritas,* but that lie from which surges beauty, that divagation toward another language, another world.

If, as Proust showed so well, childhood culinary experiences provide the paradigms that guide adult culinary pleasure and discomfort, it is also true that the culinary exists, as for Desbiolles, in a symbolic matrix far more complex than that which uses food alone as its metaphors: "I bit into the sheet to keep me from sliding into the infinitely open pit. The little bellies were quite taut, quite stuffed, quite swelled."[30] The shudder caused by an unexpected juxtaposition—that of the Pascalian theological black hole of the open pit of Hell revealed to the child during catechism contrasted to the white masses of the squid, aligned on the kitchen table many years after, perhaps strangely evoking the eucharistic host—is existential, not surreal; and the disquietude caused by recognition of one's own mortality, while not appeased by the cathartic effects of the white host, was allegorized by the squid. The hint of the abyss that spices up the squid's welcoming void is a subtle manifestation of the sublime in cuisine, a violent and scatological sublime that establishes the metaphysical piquancy of gastronomy. As Hugo reminds us in *Les travailleurs de la mer,* "All beings enter into one another. Rot is nourishment. The frightful cleansing of the globe. Man, the carnivore, is also a burier. Our lives are made of death. Such is the terrifying law. We are tombs."[31] Nothing is exempt from this law, as is proven by the eating of the gods. Indeed, for Maryline Desbiolles the essence of cuisine is "to eat death, to make it one's own, to slowly masticate it, taste it, to lick one's lips after it . . ."[32] We cook dead flesh, we cook death itself ("well spiced"), we grasp it and tear it apart with our teeth, before finally abandoning our own life to it in turn. Yet these stages of life are not chronological, and the psychological structure of life, like that of most complex narratives, is one of *hysteresis,* an anachronistic lagging of effects behind causes, the displacement of a previous influence on a subsequent response: this is precisely the structure of sublimation. "It often appeared to me, it is true, that a sensation enclosed many other, if not all, sensations, provided that it was forcefully felt."[33] Might this symbolic *mise-en-abîme* not also be the form of the culinary symbolic?

The violence of inscription, as Nietzsche revealed in *On the Genealogy of Morals,* is the source of a mnemotechnics from which cuisine is not excluded. Food takes part in the regulation and the care of the self; childhood traumas, swallowed up in the abyss of memory, are the source of a destructiveness that is none other than creativity itself. For it is upon the body and in the imagination of the narrator, as well as upon the corpses of the squid, that such mnemotechnic interventions are effected: cutting, burning, sewing. The latter operation simultaneously wounds and repairs, establishing a web of pain that articulates memory and body, text and childhood, history and cuisine: ". . . and with the aid of a kitchen thread sew the opening;"[34] ". . . one thinks of stumps whose gaping wounds had been sewn up;"[35] ". . . that we may never any longer pronounce a single word from our mouth, a mouth sewn, a mouth seamed, a mouth burnt."[36] One may well evoke at this point the philosophically cruel sewing with which D. A. F. Sade concludes *La Philosophie dans le boudoir* (Philosophy in the Bedroom, 1795), where the libertine initiate Eugénie takes a large needle and thick red thread, commanding, "Spread your thighs, Mama, and let me sew you up, so that you will give me no more brothers and sisters."[37] For Sade, this obscene and anti-genealogical gesture is an act of counter-memory, the shocking culmination of an initiatory rite that results in a perfectly sovereign and libertine individual; in *La seiche,* to the contrary, the forgetfulness announced is gentle, more sensual, more protective, for if childhood is typified in this book as the season of lilacs, it is also the perfume of this flower that causes the palliatives of forgetting.

Counter to this forgetting is the imaginary transformation of the animal-squid of the aquarium into a cooked dish; the culinary gesture is, a fortiori, a modality of remembrance. This formulation of anamnesis, as well as of the teleological expectations of desire, occurs in the ultimate scene of the book, when the work is completed and the narrator slips a ring into one of the squid, to be secretly and surprisingly transferred to the mouth of her lover as he savors the dish. Unlike the scene depicted in the famed woodblock engraving by Hokusai, *The Dream of the Fisherman's Wife* (1820)—where the woman, in full ecstasy, has her sex and mouth ravished by two octopi, in a grasp as erotic as it is terrifying—in *La seiche* the eroticism remains secret, symbolic, transformative.

Maryline Desbiolles insists, "let the end be a beginning,"[38] and, "another dish would have provided me with another tale."[39] Such are precisely the principles according to which any poetics and aesthetics of gastronomy must be based.

# 5

# Tractatus Logico-Gastronomicus

*Our taste is no longer our own, we no longer command it, it changes without our consent.*
—La Rochefoucauld, *Maximes*

Taste (culinary and otherwise) constitutes a sign of individual style, a mode of constituting the self, a mark of social position, an aesthetic gesture. While inaugurating the most intimate pleasure, cuisine simultaneously offers an incontrovertible aspect of social facade. Against the *solipsism, narcissism,* and *phantasms* of what would be the incommunicable idiosyncrasy of pure subjective taste must be counterbalanced the *communality, seduction,* and *mythology* of gastronomy. Regardless of the mode of cuisine in question—ancient, peasant, familial, bourgeoise, haute, international, nouvelle, exotic, fusion—this essay will continually fluctuate between two limits: subjective and objective, personal and interpersonal.

If every dish is a symbol, then every cuisine implies a metaphysics, all too often doomed to remain implicit. The social and aesthetic significance of a dish is most often dissimulated by the vagueries of personal "taste," buried in the dense dialectic between forgetting and anamnesis that forms and informs our senses, sensitivity, sensibility. Taste is a dynamic principle, not a static qualification or attribute, the origins of which are lost in pure contingency and escape the essentialism that haunts the other arts. Ultimately, the only manner of estimating gastronomic values and origins, of considering the question of taste, is through a "Proustian" digression: lengthy, sensual, detailed, eloquent, seductive, and most especially contingent. For our earliest culinary memories, the most archaic ones, are more ancient than paleolithic cooking, and as intimate as love.

The preference for any flavor is a function of the transmigrations, transfigurations, and reincarnations of childhood taste as it enters the public realm of culinary production and consumption, followed by transformations that continue throughout one's lifetime, sometimes conscious, often unconscious. Here, the daily habits of culinary routine simultaneously and paradoxically establish provisional limits to future gastronomic experimentation and appreciation. Taste never exists in a vacuum: it is a style like any other, organized by a selective code linking the work of farmer, merchant, chef, gourmet, and vacillating between tradition and creativity. This social "liaison" forms a hermeneutic gastronomic circle within which there always exist vestigial indications of ethics, theology, psychology, aesthetics, etiquette, magic. Thus, the question of taste is of a dense ambiguity, though not unfathomable.

The difficulty in discussing "taste" is not only due to the radical subjectiveness inherent in the cliché *de gustibus non disputandum est* (there is no disputing taste), but also in the lexical and epistemological equivocation of the word. Taste is simultaneously subjective, objective, and qualificative. According to context, *taste* means: 1. the sense by which we distinguish flavors; 2. the flavors themselves; 3. an appetite for such preferred flavors; 4. the discriminative activity according to which an individual likes or dislikes certain sensations; 5. the sublimation of such value judgments as they pertain to art, and ultimately to all experience; 6. and, by extension and ellipsis, taste implies *good* taste and style, established by means of an intuitive faculty of judgment. Yet it is precisely the figurative definition of taste, *goût,* that holds sway in quotidian discourse, defined by *Littré* as: "An entirely spontaneous faculty preceeding reflection, possessed by everybody, but which is different in each person, permitting us to appreciate the beauties and the defects in works of the spirit and in artistic productions, as taste permits us to appreciate good and bad flavors."[1]

In the *Critique of Judgement,* Kant proposes a solution to the problematic of taste (that is, the antinomy of the judgment of taste), an axiomatic ostensibly useful in attempting to answer the commonplaces posed by the tasteless: "Everyone has their own taste," and, "There is no disputing taste," or, "I don't know if it's good, but I know what I like," and, "It pleases me, therefore it is good." Kant's theory is based on the notion of a *subjective universality:* the claim that beauty functions in a rhetorical mode as a demand, establishing a universal validity that is nevertheless without any regulating concept. Taste thus becomes a universal voice speaking in the imperative mode, implying the possibility of communicating private sensations, representations, and judgments; it proffers the seemingly paradoxical universality of a singular judgment. Yet Kant's examination of judgments of taste, while being logically subtle, is rhetorically and lexically impoverished: the question of taste is in fact considerably more complex, admitting the intricacies of monologue and dialogue, rhetoric and poetry, explication and seduction, obscurity and contradiction. Kantian metaphysics must be supplemented by a historicized discourse, in order to integrate the singularities of enunciation and situation into aesthetic judgment, all the while weighing the structures of the aesthetic (culinary) object and its variegated history. *Subjective universality* must be counterbalanced by *existential historicity;* taste must indeed be discussed and disputed, as it is a profoundly dialogical form of experience.

In both Kantian metaphysics and everyday discourse, the ellipsis "taste" almost always implies "good taste," rarely "bad taste." The question of taste therefore entails the existence of a discursive community motivated by an aesthetic imperative, and not that sheer negation of value (couched in a naive relativism) so often imposed by the tasteless. Taste demands engagement, not disengagement. Thus, the argument of the fastfood lover, for exemple, who claims that taste cannot be disputed is amiss: the question of "MacDonald's" is primarily of sociological, not gastronomic, interest. While fastfood offers minor gastronomic interest, its cultural effects, to the contrary, are enormous, and pose a distinct threat to the formation of taste.[2]

Given the broadness of the meaning of "taste," the spontaneity and individuality of such judgments are but a small part of the total constituent features of taste. Subjective judgment is a phantom haunting culture and criticism. The personal, contingent, seemingly irrational origins of taste are inextricably intertwined with the social, collective, and rational structures of culture. Even as the infant struggles to speak its first words, it is already born into a linguistic system, fully formed yet mutable, infinite yet intimate, formal yet flexible. Likewise, the origins of taste in our infancy (beneath and beyond all physiological thresholds) is but the adaptation and eventual conscious transformation of the "tastes" of our parents and ancestors, of our region and country—perenially classic *and* bizarre, traditional *and* idiosyncratic.

Thus, our gastronomic points of reference—those tastes that provide the existential a prioris, the examples, paradigms, and emblems, for the development of our culinary judgment—originate in our childhood world. This is described nowhere so well as in Proust's *Du côté de chez Swann:*

> For, to a permanent background of eggs, cutlets, potatoes, jam and biscuits that she no longer even bothered to announce, Françoise added—according to the labors of the fields and the orchards, the fruits of the sea, the hazards of commerce, the kindness of neighbors and her own genius, all this done so well that our menus, like those quatrefoils sculpted on the portals of thirteenth century cathedrals, reflected somewhat the rhythms of the seasons and the stages of life: a brill because the merchant guaranteed its freshness, a turkey because she saw a beautiful one at the market of Roussainville-le-Pin, cardoons with marrow because she had never made it that way for us, a roast leg of lamb because the outdoors whetted the appetite and there

> was enough time to return for it in seven hours, spinach for a change, apricots because they were still rare, currants because in two weeks there would be no more, raspberries because Monsieur Swann specially brought them, cherries, the first from the cherry tree in two years, cottage cheese and cream because I used to like it, an almond cake because she ordered it the night before, a brioche because it was our turn to offer one.[3]

The narrator's taste literally depends upon the talents and taste of Françoise, the family's housekeeper and cook, as she transforms the world's caprices into her own. Curiously, mentioned here is only one choice specifically intended to please the narrator. Before one's individual taste becomes a matter of self-conscious thematization, choice, and development, it exists as a semiconscious selection and differentiation within the culinary field. There is a profoundly nostalgic dimension to taste; this is just as true for disgust. Yet like the deepest meanings of dreams, which always escape the dreamer, this culinary dimension is but a vague aura of ineffable pleasure and inscrutable mystery for the eater.

Separating the abundance, ostentation, and opulence of medieval and renaissance court cuisine (based on exceedingly complex accumulations, combinations, and juxtapositions of flavors and foodstuffs) from the lightness, delicacy, elegance, and near translucency of much of our contemporary cooking is the aristocratic and haute bourgeoise cuisine of the seventeenth through nineteenth centuries. Beginning in the seventeenth century with La Varenne and L. S. R., an increasing technical complexity—centered on the major technical innovation of the modern *liaison* (the use of flour to bind, or vinegar to emulsify, butter and cream sauces)—resulted in a lighter cuisine that gave particular attention to highlighting the essential qualities of individual foodstuffs. By the nineteenth century the perfection and multiplication of sauces reached their apogee (with over 150 listed by Escoffier alone), and haute cuisine received its ultimate codification by such chefs as Antonin Carême, Jules Gouffé, and Auguste Escoffier. However, the virtues of these sauces as simplifying and lightening elements were forgotten, as they found, in the hands of these very same chefs, new uses in a bourgeois cuisine of increasing heaviness, complexity, and ostentation, establishing a style that would dominate until the first inklings of a nouvelle cuisine in the 1960s.

It is precisely at those points of culinary history where simplification and rationalization result in gustatory transparency that cuisine surpasses what Philippe Gillet speaks of as a *mise-en-présence* (presentation) of foodstuffs and tastes, to achieve a modern, intrinsically culinary *mise-en-oeuvre* (preparation): fascination with appearances gives way to experimentation with gustatory qualities and essences.[4] Thus, all the major cooking techniques—roasting, boiling, stewing, frying, grilling, sautéing, steaming—are now utilized to reveal and harmonize, rather than juxtapose and distort, the original and unique flavors of the main ingredients. It is as if the taste for Renaissance *vanitas* were superceded by a desire for the *natures mortes* of Chardin, Cézanne, and the masters of Zen calligraphy. That any flavor may exist in its own glory is precisely the summit of contemporary cooking; as Jean-François Revel explains, "[T]he summits of the art are attained precisely in those periods where the refinement of recipes associates a complexity of conception with the lightness of results."[5] Complexity of conception provides the range of variations on a theme that permit continual inventiveness; lightness of realization assures the presentation of the essential, primal qualities of foodstuffs, harkening back to the nostalgia for simple flavors raised to their quintessential powers. Essence dominates appearance.

Modernist art and modern cuisine have long held a central trope in common: *invention.* Indeed, even simplification is a mode of invention. If there were to be a theorization of cuisine, it would constitute a theory of exceptions, nuances, refinements. Culinary taste would transform aesthetics by redefining the role of art within the human sensorium, transforming the aestheticization of the senses and eliminating the previously held limits between the arts. The gastronomic must no longer serve as mere metaphor for the arts, but should take its place with the muses.

The modernist conditions of cuisine must be placed in a historical context, insofar as they reveal a startling coincidence between the nouvelle cuisine and the discourses of modernism and postmodernism in the arts, both of which share several central tenets: *self-conscious reflexivity* (experimentation to reveal the primary qualities of the component materials of a work); *questioning of origins* (the realization that all inventions are but variations, transmutations, or inspirations based on previous works); *regionalism* (the decentralization and relativization of techniques, materials, and styles); *exoticism and fusion* (the juxtaposition and incorporation of foreign elements on equal footing with native material). Indeed, if we consider postmodernism to have chronologically followed the late-1960s movements of minimalism and conceptualism, then we may consider the French nouvelle cuisine, originating at approximately the same moment, as a true aesthetic avant-garde. We cannot be blind to such stylistic innovations and conceptual complications, to these coincidences and intersections, if we are to enhance our appreciation of contemporary cuisine in relation to the other arts—and vice versa.

As contemporary cuisine tends to highlight and accentuate the natural flavors of a dish's isolated main aliment, subsidiary flavorings tend to become more and more subtle, consisting of just what is needed to heighten, rather than transform or dissimulate, the central flavor. Thus the operative terms for the use of condiments are *un rien, un soupçon, une touche, une idée* (a nothing, a suspicion, a touch, an idea). Curiously, these are all philosophical notions that, if juxtaposed in a somewhat surreal manner, would entail not mimesis but counter-mimesis: for what would the *touch of an idea* or a *suspicion of nothingness?* In a rhetorical gesture intended to give rise to discourse, taste would be constituted simultaneously by: recognition of typicality; judgment of quality; choice of style—recognitions, judgments and choices often operative at infinitesmal levels of determination. Taste as discrimination must be differentiated from taste as appreciation, even though the former is a necessary precondition of the latter. It might thus be fruitful to consider the question of taste according to a structural analysis, so as to contextualize the possibilities of choice without eliminating the problematic of idiosyncrasy. In this way, the issue of taste may be explained in terms of the constitution of pertinent factors in a differential system. An appropriate model might be the semiotic analysis of colors, which, mutatis mutandis, offers valuable insights concerning the confluence of those subjective, objective, and cultural values that constitute perception.[6] The differences between identification and discrimination, appreciation and preference, must be considered. The eye can discriminate many more colors (nearly ten million!) than can be named; taste too is exceedingly complex, where the five basic gustatory qualities of which all flavors are constituted (bitter, sour, salty, sweet, neutral) appear in infinite variation. The manner in which the naming of the visible spectrum (schematized as red, orange, yellow, green, blue, indigo, violet) groups and limits these differences is not only the discursive foundation of all chromatic symbolism, but is also a factor in the effective reduction of color discrimination. The extremes of describing color would be either the subjective literary recollection of contingent appearance, or an objective statement of wavelength; while the latter would be incapable of taking into account all of the subsidiary (and often synaesthetic) aspects of the lived context that co-determines the appreciation of color, the former always entails imprecision and ambiguity, permitting a certain range of interpretation—both often entail color-blindness.

The need for precise description or nomination is well known to wine tasters: the creation of a specialized vocabulary—however pretentious it may seem to the uninitiated—is necessary for both the communication and discrimination of flavors. *Aggressive, sharp, amorous, ample, amusing, aqueous, ardent, aristocratic, austere, balsamic, brilliant, brusque, coaxing, caressing, solid, charged, structured, delicate, discreet, distinguished, elegant, worn, blooming, bland, feminine, fine, melting, foxy, gay, heavy, herbaceous, formless, liqueurous, long, thin, soft, rounded, nervous, clean, noble, unctuous, open, closed, perfidious, little, pinching, powerful, pure, round, rough, severe, solid, supple, suave, tender, tranquil, sad, velvety, old.*[7] This highly abbreviated, and vastly heterogeneous, list is only a sample; furthermore, such qualifiers shift in significance for each type of wine described. The palate—of colors, of tastes—is always circumscribed by the limits of description. When Toulouse-Lautrec claimed that a good wine should be "like a peacock's tail in the mouth," he meant it both in qualitative terms, as a beautiful burst of color-flavor, and in quantitative terms, an all-encompassing, complex coloration, containing the entire spectrum. Hyperbole helps us escape the limitations of language! Jean Dubuffet explains this phenomenon in a particularly Nietzschean mode:

> And yet we also have the feeling that the repertory of words utilized in each of our languages is extremely narrow in relation to the innumerable apprehensions of thought, and that each of these words suffers a great poverty in their abstract status, in order to translate the particular situations of each designated thing and the associations that link thought to it. It is said that there are fifteen different ways of saying "camel" in Arab, and there are without a doubt as many ways of saying "seal" or "snow" in Eskimo. But do only fifteen suffice? A hundred times a hundred thousand are needed. And in this regard, we still wouldn't

> have enough. For thought is in motion, while words are inert bodies. What we need is words in motion.[8]

The matter is reduced to its simplest terms in the joke about the man who claims that he can, without fail, identify any wine in the world. Blindfolded, he is put to the test by his friends. Offered a glass, he takes a sip and proudly proclaims: "Red!" Certainly, the more differential qualities one looks for, the better one may judge, and the higher the level of connoisseurship. Though the nature of quotidian discourse on wine rarely takes on the specialization of professional tastings, judgments nevertheless vary according to the level of competency regarding complexity. The more specific the categorization, the more subtle need be the qualifications: red / white; Bordeaux / Burgundy; Médoc / Graves; Haut-Médoc / Médoc; Pauillac / St.-Julien; Mouton-Rothschild / Lafite-Rothschild; Mouton-Rothschild 1966 / Mouton-Rothschild 1970; Mouton-Rothschild 1966 tasted in 1979 / Mouton-Rothschild 1966 tasted in 1999. The narrower the range of objects, the greater the need for qualification, description, differentiation. It happens that in contemporary appreciation of wine, complexity is highly valued (nothwithstanding the phenomenon of the *vins nouveaux*). Yet it should be apparent that every type of wine (though hardly every bottle) has its own virtue, as well as its place in a respective cuisine. The domain of wine is one where superlatives abound, and one might venture that as long as a single fulcrum for quality exists, a qualitative culinary discourse remains possible. For many, such an "absolute" is represented by Château d'Yquem (the most famous and most appallingly expensive Sauternes), regarded as the quintessence of perfection and complexity. Michel Serres in *Les cinq sens* articulates the depth structure of this wine's taste: wild rose, lilac, clematis, early summer fruit, peach, pear, apple, grape, walnut, hazlenut, fern, truffle, humus, resin; rare fragrances, minerals, silex, flint; animal odors, musk, amber, wet fur, love sweat; etherial undertones of acetone; aromatics such as mint, geranium; ambrosias, jasmin, vanilla, linden; balms such as benzoin, daisy, camphor; empyreumas such as coffee, tobacco.[9] Even so, this description falls short of the wine's stupendously intricate, indeed labyrinthine, taste. In fact, d'Yquem is a monster of perfection, a hybrid ontological intermingling of the three kingdoms (animal, vegetable, mineral), connecting heaven and earth (meteorologically and botanically) in a gustatory intricacy so profound that it ultimately defies description.

It is precisely in wine tasting (where the sheer numerical and stylistic possibilities of invention are relatively circumscribed in relation to those of cooking) that we may establish a combinatory grid that permits the sort of subtle and precise determinations that may inform connoisseurship. For to combine the results of horizontal tastings (several vintages of a single wine; a diachronic analysis) and vertical tastings (several wines of a single vintage, usually limited to one town or region; a synchronic analysis) would be to taste wines not against personal preferences, nor against appropriate foods, but rather within a range of related wines, such that typicality may be delimited. Yet it must be stressed that this grid itself is unstable; as each wine ages to a point of perfection, sooner or later it declines in quality; the palate is transformed with age and disease; preferences change with knowledge and experience; and culinary aesthetics, regarding both wine and food, shifts with styles and epochs. Whence the crucial role of memory in taste: one need not only be able to differentiate according to increasingly subtle criteria, but also to remember and mentally contrast those typical gustatory characteristics that make such differentiation possible. Yet the selectiveness of memory creates both identities and differences: for the chef, what is crucial is how a recipe is transformed into one's own. Culinary idiosyncrasy is the vanguard of progress; the recipe is not a canon, code, or regulation, and the typicality or "authenticity" of a dish is but a range of possibilities, an indeterminate ideal, a pole of transformations.

Qualifications of taste (as sensual discrimination, aesthetic judgment, critical appreciation) are not simply physiological, psychological, or aesthetic: they are also symbolic, insofar as the discriminations of taste are filtered through language. Appreciation demands discrimination; discrimination presupposes appreciation. This does not imply that only those tastes that are named are experienced, but rather more broadly that language establishes and foregrounds gustatory relations, kinships, limits, determinations, specifications, nuances. Nomination is both a trap and a guide. As the common name of a single species of plant or animal changes from region to region, its taste also changes, due to both terrestrial and linguistic shifts. Differences in taste may be dissimulated as well as revealed by language and culture: such determinations are made according to the manner in which the global system of taste relations (in a given culture and cuisine) are established by a continual sedimentation of gustatory references and cross-references. The combination of foodstuffs parallels the the case of phonemes in a given language: all combinations of sounds are possible, though relatively few make sense.

The lexical imprint on the semantic field may be the cause of regional and even national blind spots regarding taste, as well as of the creation of false discriminations and determinations. These complications may be caused by *inadequacy of word to taste* (which is the case for the vast majority of unnamed nuances); *inadequacy of taste to word* (for example, my own blind spot regarding truffles, the much vaunted taste of which remains a mystery to me, even after repeated efforts); or *lexical ambiguity* (which entails, or reveals, confusions of taste). A case in point might be useful. I continuously have arguments in France about the relationship between two related though distinct herbs, which in English are differentiated as *dill* (normally, in French, *aneth*) and *fennel (fenouil)*. These are botanically differentiated respectively as the species *Anethum graveolus* and *Foeniculum vulgare,* both of the family *Umbelliferae.* While many people in France argue that they are either the same thing or else minor variations of the same herb, I, with Polish and

Hungarian origins—cultures where dill is widely used, and fennel relatively unappreciated—can not only differentiate between the two, but have as great an aversion to fennel and anis as I have a taste for dill. The cause of this Gallic equivocation is complex. Visually nearly identical, *aneth* and *fenouil* are in fact defined in a confusing manner by the major French dictionaries:

1. *Le Petit Robert* defines *fenouil* (*fenouil doux* [sweet fennel]) as *feniculum* of the family *Ombelliféracées,* referring in the same entry to *aneth* (*fenouil amer* [bitter fennel]) without any further botanical specification; the entry for *aneth,* in turn, simply refers the reader to *fenouil.* Thus, the two appear to be synonymous, with a minor variation specifically marked in terms of a categorical variation of taste (sweet/bitter).
2. The *Littré* is somewhat more precise, yet also ambiguous: *fenouil* is defined as *anethum foeniculum* of the family *Ombellifères,* while *fenouil bâtard* [bastard fennel] is defined as *anethum graveolens;* all the while, *aneth* is given no more precision that that of being a *plante ombellifère.* According to these definitions, the two may be different, though not necessarily.
3. *Harrap's New Standard French and English Dictionary* translates *fenouil* as *fennel, fenouil officinal* as *sweet fennel,* and *fenouil bâtard* as *dill;* in turn, *aneth* is translated as *anethum, aneth odorant* as *dill,* and *aneth doux* as *fennel.* In the other direction, *fennel* is translated as both *fenouil* and *aneth doux,* while *dill* is translated as both *aneth odorant* and *fenouil bâtard.* Here, perhaps thanks to the non-French origin of the text, the two are at least differentiated, albeit still muddled. The continual association, indeed confusion, between the two plants is based on botanical family resemblance, not on species (or even taste) differentiation. Obviously, a precise determination is of great culinary import. As would be said in linguistics, a disambiguification is needed.

Clearly, the extremely limited culinary use value of these herbs in France hardly motivated, until recently, a well-defined linguistic differentiation: dill has not been a pertinent feature of classic French cuisine, as it has been in the Baltic countries. But this situation is fated to change, as the culinary lexicon is being pressured from two sides: first, the increased internationalism of gastronomy and the contemporary fashion of fusion cuisine demands a more precise vocabulary and accurate translations; second, research into ancient, medieval, and Renaissance cuisine (where variants of these plants were abundantly used) demands equal precision, one already inherent in the Latin distinctions between species, genus, and family. These distinctions are slowly passing into everyday French usage. Indeed, one notes the increasing presence of dill on French tables, linked precisely to the current popularity of smoked and marinated fish dishes.

Taste (as discrimination of flavor) is a function of refinement: empirical tastes (flavors) are determined and organized according to cultural meanings and usages. Gastronomic tradition is a symbolic system dependant upon the pertinentization of specific objects within the system; conversely, gastronomic creativity establishes new pertinent features, and thus transforms the system itself. The determination of what constitutes pertinent factors within any given gastronomic discourse is precisely at the origin of the gastronomic symbolic: by transgressing prescribed thresholds between flavor determinations, their uses, and use-values, a culinary allusion may be transformed into a gastronomic essence. To enlarge the field of differentiation and to make categories more subtle, malleable, and permeable is to improve taste, and thus to consequently elaborate the codes of taste. This is precisely the role of the specialist, both chef and gastronome, since polemic—whether between chef and chef, chef and gourmet, or gourmet and critic—is necessary for the advancement of cuisine as a fine art. To escape the limits of the given gastronomic rules of an epoch is to enrich the field of taste (flavor and quality). As new pertinent features are foregrounded (the possibility of differentiating fennel and dill, for example), there evolves a discovery of dishes based on these acquired tastes, such as the Russian *beef stroganoff* (slices of beef in a cream and mustard sauce with dill). Though the addition of dill in this dish is not always called for in Russian recipes, its use establishes the dish as all the more distinctive. Indeed, one of my favorite Paris restaurants, Le Hangar, emblematizes this situation by making an excellent beef stroganoff, though, perhaps as a concession to French taste, the dill is eliminated; needless to say, I resist the temptation, for this particular variation poses a definite gustatory lack for my palate. Nevertheless, the possibility of the intrusion of dill upon the French palate redefines certain affinities between herbs, sauces, and meats, such that the nature of the entire system changes by the expansion and reorientation of acceptable relationships between terms. Here, the art of gastronomy is to reveal and name hitherto unknown nuances, indeed to discover entirely unknown dishes and cuisines.

It is one thing to create such complex taste grids and structural gastronomic combinations; it is another to form a taste, a culinary style (whether as chef, gourmet, or writer). Style is a function of what the philosopher Maurice Merleau-Ponty referred to as "coherent deformation," which implies the existence of a series of transfigurations within a normative system: not creativity versus tradition, but creativity *informed* by tradition and tradition *transformed* by creativity. One must always wonder, when reading a restaurant review or a recipe, precisely what motivated the writer to order and write about any given dish.

In terms of culinary creativity, each epoch has its paradigmatic realm of invention. In this regard, the salad may be considered a veritable ontological transformer in the nouvelle cuisine. As Claude Fischler explains in *L'homnivore,* "The salad will impose itself as a territory of superlative freedom, of a more or less considered madness. It is by definition the domain of melange and organized disorder. It therefore escapes from traditional culinary grammars, and henceforth permits unhindered transgression and innovation."[10] It is generally considered that this freedom-in-salads was inaugurated, in its nouvelle cuisine version, by Michel Guérard, and Jacques Manière even named his own a *salade folle* (mad salad). However, before 1975 no starred Michelin restaurant listed in the guidebook a salad among its specialities; the first to do so, in that year, were Alain Chapel with a *Salade de homard* (lobster salad) and Jacques Pic with a *Salade de pêcheurs au xérès* (fisherman's salad with sherry).[11] The dialectic between the indigenous and the exotic is a key factor in both modernist and postmodernist art, cuisine included; as in poetry, the constant tension between the limits of the familiar and the effects of creative defamiliarization mark the boundaries of the culinary possibilities of an epoch. Consider one of the creations of Alain Senderens, who was instrumental in helping establish the nouvelle cuisine by integrating foreign techniques and recipes into French cooking, as well as by rediscovering long-lost recipes from ancient, medieval, and Renaissance sources. At his former Parisian restaurant, L'Archestrate, one of his masterpieces was a particularly luscious salad: *Salade de homard aux mangues et basilic* (lobster and mango salad with basil). The question as to whether this dish was inspired by or merely homologous to the traditional Vietnamese papaya and shrimp salad with lemongrass is a moot point. Senderens's salad is rendered de luxe by substituting lobster for shrimp, and it is gallicized (via Provence) by substituting basil and vinaigrette for lemonweed and the fermented fish sauce *nuac mam*. Crucial is both the manner in which such salads stretch the limits of what constitutes a "salad" in France, and the inspiration that such an influx of exotic flavors offers for other creations, such as Senderens's more recent *Homard à la vanille* (vanilla lobster).

In counterdistinction to the domestication of the exotic, we may also consider the question of typicality in terms of the renovation of the indigenous. Formerly, at the Restaurant Chantecler of the Hôtel Negresco in Nice, the then head chef Dominique Le Stanc foreshadowed his brilliant transformations of regional cuisine—such as the *Risotto aux artichauts, parmesan et râpée de truffes noires* (risotto with artichokes, parmesan, and shaved black truffles) or the *Fricassée de St-Jacques et langoustines au basilic* (fricassee of sea scallops and scampi with basil)—with the offering of a fanciful appetizer: a lilliputian *pan bagnat.* This sandwich, typically niçois but for its size, small as the tip of one's thumb, offered all the archetypical flavors (tuna, crudités, olives, olive oil) condensed into one bite—all the more amusing because once a year, on the beach opposite the hotel, one of the popular, if grotesque, attractions of this city is the creation of a gargantuan *pan bagnat* one kilometer long!

I have met a person—cultivated, equilibrious, sane, aesthete—who often quite simply cannot decide what to eat. His indecision is such that it almost paralyzes him. To resolve the situation, he enters a supermarket, chooses a customer at random, and follows that person, placing into his shopping cart all the same things chosen by the other. Like a "man without qualities" living according to the surrealist ideal of objective chance, he instantiates the depressing contemporary commonplace of conditioned, stereotyped, limited taste. In a consumer society of the spectacle, his comportment reveals precisely why for many, *taste is the discourse of the other.* It is only through a combination of knowledge and pleasure, of connoisseurship and discovery, that we can make it our own.

## Postface

# An Introduction to Modern French Cuisine through Several Exemplary Menus

> *There must, for me at least, be a faint nebular madness, dignified no matter how deliberate, to a dinner that is exquisite.*
> —M. F. K. Fisher, *An Alphabet for Gourmets*

Philippe Gillet, in *Le goût et les mots,* (Taste and Words) suggests that "The true gastronomic literature is hidden in cookbooks,"[1] since the most eloquent commentary on cuisine consists in the written recipes themselves. I would add that menus—which belong to the ontological category of prophetic phenomena and, like most prophesies, disappoint more often than not—are occasionally equally revelatory and seductive. Consequently, I offer the following schematic history—obviously skewed by my taste—to modern French cuisine.

Grimod de la Reynière, "Le souper funèbre" (funeral supper), Paris, 1783[2]

*Soupe à la tortue*
*Pains de seigle russe*
*Olives de Turquie*
*Caviar*
*Poutarges de mulets*
*Boudins fumés de Francfort*

*Gibiers aux sauces couleur de jus de réglisse et de cirage*
*Coulis de truffes*
*Crèmes ambrées au chocolat*
*Poudings*
*Brugnons, raisins, mûres, guignes*

Every epoch, every social group, has its own forms of ostentation, culinary and otherwise. It would be difficult to write of gastronomy without mention of decadence, for excess and ostentation are of the essence of haute cuisine and food has always been among the most common forms of conspicuous consumption. It should therefore not go unnoticed that one of the foundational moments in the history of modern cuisine was one of its most decadent meals: Grimod de la Reynière's mock funerary feast, an extended joke highlighting a banquet of all black foods in a particularly morbid setting. Indeed, it was deemed so perverse that Huysmans, in *À rebours* [Against the Grain], the nineteenth-century exemplar of decadence, used it as the model for his character des Esseintes's final feast.

French haute cuisine had always stressed the decorative, from the extravagances of the great court feasts through the *pièces montées* at the center of Carême's incipient modernism. That I have chosen to begin with this all-black meal is not by chance, for the two versions (Grimod's and Huysmans's) span precisely the century in which modern cuisine originated and was ultimately codified and institutionalized. In Huysmans, the pleasure and surprise inherent in Grimod's culinary theater was subverted and transformed, revealing the rarely cited underside of gastronomy, that morbidity and mortality which is the key to all *vanitas.* For Grimod, the black meal was advance publicity for a life that would be devoted to the sensual pleasures; for Huysmans, it would mark the beginning of a fin-de-siècle ascetisism at the service of aesthetic sensitivity, literary creativity, and religious preoccupations. Perhaps the combination of these two positions defines the gastronomic art, which is as much an intellectual as a sensual practice, one where decadence—in the form of extreme, even baroque sophistication—is often a key factor in culinary creativity.

D. A. F. Sade, "Dîner fort irritant" (A most exciting dinner), Charenton, 1804[3]

*Potage au bouillon de vingt-quatre petits moineaux,*
*fait au riz et au safran*
*Une tourte dont les boulettes sont de viande de pigeon hachée et*
*garnie de culs d'artichauts*
*Une crème à la vanille*
*Des truffes à la provençale*
*Une dinde garnie de truffes*
*Des oeufs au jus*
*Un hachis de blanc de perdrix farci de truffes et vin cuit*
*Vin de Champagne*
*Une compote à l'ambre*

The aphrodisiacal nature of this menu—composed while Sade was interned in the psychiatric asylum of Charenton—is apparent (truffles, champagne, ambergris), as is its Provençal flavor. Sade's gastronomic sensibility was formed by several factors: his Provençal origins (his family owned three chateaux in Provence, including his own beloved one at La Coste in the Lubéron); his high aristocratic heritage; and his superlatively erotic imagination. And yet, this menu is particularly modern, and can well be imagined, with very few changes, in a restaurant such as Chênes Verts at Tourtour (Var, France), specializing in truffled dishes. One might well imagine that Sade's culinary phantasms were as precise as his erotic ones, and that this menu truly represents his gastronomic passions.

Chez Véry, 1814[4]

*Écrevisses*
*Perdrix aux choux*

*Ris de veau à l'oseille*
*Fèves du marais à la crème*
*Cerises de Montmorency*

This is the meal I would have chosen from the extensive 1814 menu of Véry, one of most exclusive Parisian restaurants of the epoch; most of the dishes would be familiar to diners in today's Parisian bistrots. Such a choice gives an idea of the newfound possibilities of the menu *à la russe* (that is, with dishes served consecutively, as opposed to the menu *à la française,* with numerous dishes served simultaneously). I chose the crayfish because of the near impossibility of obtaining uncultivated ones in France today; the partridge with cabbage because it is a dish I enjoy cooking, and would thus like to compare versions; the sweetbreads in sorrel simply because I like the dish (and, given the current health scares in Europe related to the inner organs of cattle, I would now prefer to eat this dish in the imagination); the fava beans in cream because I'm fascinated by the symbolism of the *fève* and its ritualistic use in French culture (notably regarding the *galette des Roi* and the feast of the Epiphany); and the Montmorency cherries because they have almost completely disappeared: I once had the pleasure of tasting some, from a friend's family garden, preserved in alcohol.

Antonin Carême, Château au Bois de Boulogne
(for twelve guests), 6 July 1829[5]

Deux Potages:
*Le potage à la Condé*
*Le potage à la moelle de boeuf*
Deux Relevés de Poisson:
*Le bar grillé à l'italienne*
*Le cabillaud à la hollandaise*
Deux Grosses Pièces:
*Le quartier d'agneau à l'anglaise*
*La chartreuse garnie de cailles*

Quatre Entrées:
*Les petits vol-au-vent à la Nesle*
*L'émincé de filets de boeuf à la Clerment*
*La poularde à la maquignon*
*Les filets de lapereaux glacés à la chicorée*
Deux Plats de Rôt:
*Les poulets à la reine*
*Les pigeons bardés*
Deux Relevés de Plats de Rôt:
*Le croque-en-bouche à la moderne*
*La sultane en surprise*
Quatre Entremets:
*Les haricots blancs à la maître d'hôtel*
*Les laitues braisées au consommé*
*La gelée d'abricots renversée*
*Les fanchonnettes au café moka*

That this menu for a summer feast might be slightly misrepresented in the account of Lady Morgon is beside the point, since it fully captures the style and dimension of Carême's feasts. Despite Carême's protestations to the contrary, this menu is hardly modern, being typical of a post-Restauration aristocratic dinner *à la française.* That Carême was never constrained to work in a restaurant—having been the private chef of Talleyrand, the King of England, the Emperors of Russia and Austria, and Baron Rothschild—certainly explains his predilection for an ostentatious and excessive cuisine. The roots of his menus were firmly planted in the aristocratic tradition of the Ancien Régime, however forward looking the specifics of his recipes might have been, in terms of both the simplification of dishes and the elimination of the *repas en ambigu* (sweetness and saltiness combined in the same dishes and the same courses). It is telling that, while being one of the greatest chefs in French history, he is remembered, at least in the popular imagination, nearly as much for his extravagant *pièces montées* as for his cuisine. In cuisine, the visual aspect of a *pièce montée* very often surpasses the gastronomic value of the dish itself, however antithetical this might seem regarding the gustatory goals of cooking. For the most celebrated of French chefs, Carême, the decorative values of cuisine always existed on an equal level with its gustatory qualities. Indeed, Carême's decorative perfectionism often transcended his culinary aspirations, as in the use of inedible binding materials to guarantee the longevity of certain *pièces montées.* Carême, the architectural autodidact whom one gastronome referred to as "The Palladio of Cuisine," spent untold hours studying drawing, architecture, and garden design (notably works on garden follies) in the *cabinet des estampes* of the Bibliothèque Nationale. This is fully attested to by his volumes *Le Patissier Pittoresque* (1815) and *Le Patissier Royal Parisien* (1815), where the art of pastry reached its mimetic apotheosis. While Carême's culinary inventions and simplifications hastened the modern transformation of cuisine, his continuing passion for complex place settings and extravagant pastry decorations was already anachronistic.

Balzac, Chez Véry, circa 1834[6]

*Hors-d'oeuvres*
*100 huîtres d'Ostende*
*12 côtelettes de pré-salé au naturel*
*Un caneton aux navets*
*Une paire de perdreaux rôtis*
*Une sole normande*
*Fruits*
*Poires de doyenne*

Even given what might be a slight exaggeration, manifesting the ressentiment of a publisher regarding his author, the meal was nevertheless most probably genuine, given Balzac's gargantuan appetite. However, for the classic expression of the hyperbolic in culinary literature, the reader is directed to Rabelais himself; the former stretches the stomach, the latter the imagination.

Dinner of the Three Emperors (Prussia, Russia, China),
Café Anglais, 7 June 1867[7]

*Potage Impératrice*
*Potage Fontanges*
*Soufflés à la Reine*
*Filets de sole à la vénitienne*
*Escalopes de turbot au gratin*
*Selle de mouton, purée bretonne*
*Poulets à la portugaise*
*Pâté chaud de cailles*
*Homards à la parisienne*
*Sorbets au vin*
*Canetons à la rouennaise*
*Ortolans sur canapés*
*Aubergines à l'espagnole*
*Asperges en branches*
*Cassolette Princesse*
*Bombe glacée*

The *bombe glacée* finale must have incited great hilarity on the part of the anarchists of the day.

Café Voisin, 25 December 1870 (ninety-ninth day of the siege of the Paris commune)[8]

*Tête d'âne farcie*
*Consommé d'éléphant*
*Chameau rôti à l'anglaise*
*Civet de kangourou*
*Côtes d'ours rôties sauce poivrade*

*Cuissot de loup sauce chevreuil*
*Chat flanqué de rats*
*Terrine d'antilope aux truffes*

One might compare that great ellipsis, that nonrepresentation, of a feast in the wedding scene of Victor Hugo's *Les misérables,* where, in the joyous culmination of the tale (related to the July Monarchy uprisings), food is never once mentioned! Indeed, given the penury that shapes the moral texture of the narrative—epitomized by the famed scene where a young bourgeois feeds bread to the birds in the Luxembourg Gardens while the starving protagonist looks on—any hint of hedonism in the feast would appear as an ethical lapse. In any case, with the incorporation of exotic foods into French cuisine in the early twentieth century (at least into specialty shops such as Corcellet) partly as a result of the new trends introduced at the International Expositions, some of the dishes on this menu would become acceptable, if hardly standard, European fare. (I have eaten kangaroo, for example, in Australia, served in a matter-of-fact manner in a quite sophisticated restaurant; ostrich farming now even exists in France.) Abjection in cuisine is culturally relative, and the formation of taste is structured as much by societal prohibitions and prescriptions as by physiological and aesthetic thresholds. The rat, to take an extreme example, is eaten, outside of moments of starvation, in approximately forty-two cultures.[9]

Stéphane Mallarmé, menu of a hunting luncheon,
20 September 1874[10]

*Harengs salés*
*Saucisson de Paris (Duthé)*
*Beurre du pays*
*Terrine de levraut à l'ancienne*
*Perdreaux gris piqués froids à la gelée*
*Filet de boeuf en Bellevue*

*Brioche mousseline*
*Gelée de groseilles de Bar*
*Fromage de Sept-Moncel ou du pays et fruits*

It would be difficult to discern something "mallarméian" about this menu —invented by Mallarmé for his fashion magazine, *La dernière mode,* for which he wrote, pseudonymously, all the articles—except for the *mousseline;* attempts to relate this meal to his poetry are seemingly futile. Perhaps this may serve as a lesson that the intentional fallacy operates in gastronomic as well as in literary analysis.

Banquet for the Mayors of France (22,695 guests),
Jardin des Tuileries, 22 September 1900[11]

*Hors-d'oeuvre*
*Darnes de Saumon glacées Parisienne*
*Filet de Boeuf en Bellevue*
*Pains de canetons de Rouen*
*Poulardes de Bresse rôties*
*Ballotines de faisans Saint-Hubert*
*Salade Potel*
*Glaces Succès.—Condés*
*Dessert*

The total amount of food consumed in this culinary representation of French democracy included 1,800 ducklings, 2,500 chickens, 2,430 pheasants, 2,000 kilos of salmon, 2,400 kilos of beef, 2,500 liters of green beans, kidney beans, potatoes, celery, 10,000 peaches, 1,000 kilos of grapes, 1,200 liters of mayonnaise, and 700 jars of mustard. Just as haute cuisine in the hands of Carême passed from Talleyrand to Rothschild—from the exceedingly aristocratic to the hyperbolically bourgeois—the other major strand of its cultural destiny in nineteenth-century France was in the hands of the petite bourgeoisie, where excess began to be manifested in quantitative and statistical, rather than anecdotic, truths. The inner tension in the gastronomic existence of many francophilic food lovers consists in the conflict between the rooted regionalism of peasant and bourgeois cooking as opposed to the increasing internationalism of haute cuisine, with all the attendant symbolic and cultural implications of these differences. The assembly of all the mayors of France at this Parisian banquet was intended as a symbol of both the purported integrity of the Republic and the unity of "French" cuisine; in fact, the French Republic and French cuisine are both but palimpsests and mosaics of numerous traditions, cultures, and histories, as varied as the different patois that mark France's linguistic diversity.

Escoffier, Christmas menu, 1903[12]

*Crêpe aux oeufs de Sterlet*
*Consommé Santa-Maria*
*Velouté aux Paillettes dorées*
*Paupiette de Sole sous la cendre*
*Caille à l'Orientale*
*Jeune Chevreuil aux Cerises*
*Crème de Marrons*
*Suprême de Foie gras au Champagne*
*Neige aux Perles des Alpes*
*Chapon accompagné d'Ortolans Ste. Alliance*
*Salade Nazareth*
*Asperges de France*
*Le plum pudding des Trois Mages*
*L'Étoile au Berger*
*Bénédictins Blancs*

Auguste Escoffier was, at the turn of the century, the pivotal figure in French cuisine: he catalogued and codified haute cuisine in his *Le guide culinaire* (1903), a work that would remain the foundational French cookbook until the inception of the nouvelle cuisine in the 1960s. His association with César Ritz, the international hotel magnate—the origin of the word *ritzy*—helped assure the French basis of international haute cuisine. It wasn't until the advent of the nouvelle cuisine that the inverse effect would occur, that is, the full-scale influx of foreign aliments and techniques into French cuisine. Note the theological allusions of certain dishes on this menu.

Marcel Proust, Dinner chez Madame Verdurin
*(Du côté de chez Swann)*[13]

*Salade "Francillon"*
*Écrevisses grillées*
*Sole à la normande*
*Salade*
*Mousse de fraises*

I could have chosen a madeleine and tea—or even a cold beer—as the preferred Proustian meal, but that would suggest more about the existential particularities of the narrator and author, rather atypical figures, than of the disappearing social milieu which it was his passion to describe.

Dinner to celebrate the birth of Marcel Proust,
Hôtel Ritz, Paris, July 1971[14]

*Crème Argenteuil*
*Sole normande*
*Boeuf en gelée*
*Salade de truffes et d'ananas*
*Sorbet au thé*
*Madeleines*

That this meal, a compilation of the most celebrated dishes from the *Recherche,* took place at the Hôtel Ritz in Paris—from which, at the end of his life, Proust used to order fried fish and cold beer to go—was a delicate if obvious touch.

Guillaume Apollinaire, Dîner gastro-astronomiste,
Lons-le-Saunier, September 1912[15]

*Violettes fraîches privées de leur tige et assaisonnées de jus de citron*
*Lottes de rivière cuites dans une décoction de feuilles d'eucalyptus*
*Faux filet saignant assaisonné de tabac à priser*
*Cailles bardées cuites dans un jus de réglisse*
*Salade assaisonnée à l'huile de noix et à la vieille eau-de-vie de marc*
*Reblochon assaisonné de noix de muscade râpé*
*Fruits de la saison*

The ambitiously and elaborately avant-garde nature of this menu—which Apollinaire himself refers to as "La cuisine nouvelle"—in fact bears many features in common with some of the most extreme and exciting inventions of the nouvelle cuisine of our times: the violets recall the use of the same flower by Michel Bras; the role of eucalyptus leaves is similar to wrapping techniques utilizing banana leaves or algae, derived from Thai and Japanese cuisine, and is also akin to Bras's dessert of apple compote with red and black currants served in a gentian leaf; the curiosity of chewing tobacco as flavoring is not unlike Pierre Gagnaire's use of whole coffee beans in a sauce or Alain Hacquard's (Lapérouse) use of ground coffee to cure salmon; licorice flavoring has become quite common (remember its considerably more dramatic use in Grimod's funeral meal); salad dressings utilizing unusual oils and fruit vinegars are the rage; and the taste for relatively exotic (or at least rarely used, in the modern context) spices, such as nutmeg, is ever increasing, as exemplified by the cooking of Olivier Roellinger. Insofar as the dishes described are eminently edible, this experimental meal bears little gastronomic comparison with the otherwise avant-garde Marinetti and Fillìa publication, *La cucina futurista* (Futurist Cuisine), which includes, for example, a dessert called a "Libyan Airplane," consisting of glazed chestnuts marinated first in *eau de Cologne* and then in milk, served on a paté of bananas, apples, dates and sweet peas in the form of an airplane.[16] This "cuisine" appears more phantasmagoric and contentious than gastronomic, and seems to bear a closer relation to the Futurist plastic arts than to the history of cuisine. Or, just perhaps, we have simply not caught up with the genius of their culinary imagination.

Raymond Roussel, menu of October 1926[17]

*Framboises au sucre*
*Soupe au chocolat*
*Fromage bondon*
*Huîtres royales marines*
*Talmouses de Saint-Denis au brie de Meaux*
*Filets de merlan à l'anglaise,*
*beurre noisette, persil frit*
*Cailles au foie gras à la Cambacérès,*
*compote de raisin de chasselas de Thomery au coulis*
*Noisette de Béhague à la Doria*
*Sorbet au Champagne*
*Coeur de filet à la broche*
*Pommes soufflées*
*Salade de laitue*
*Pêche impératrice Eugénie*
*Religieuse au café*
*Bombe Nélusko*
*Consommé Monte-Carlo, crème princesse*
*Vol-au-vent de filet de sole Walewska*
*Suprême de perdreau souveraine*
*Spoom*
*Poulet de grain à la broche*
*Salade caprice de reine*
*Ananas voilé à l'orientale*

Raymond Roussel fancied raspberries. Every day during the height of the summer season, one of his Rolls-Royces descended toward his property in the Alpes-Maritimes, while another returned to Paris, bearing a small basket of the precious fruit. Like the emblem on his letterhead—the "RR" of his initials reversed and interlaced in specular echo—the "RR" on the radiator of the first Rolls would find its mirror image in the redoubled "RR" of the second one, as they crossed paths, in palindromic elegance, halfway between Roussel's properties in Neuilly and the South. These raspberries, his own, were consequently the most expensive imaginable. They fulfilled a stylistic condition, indeed an axiomatics, of Roussel's poetics: to transform the quotidian into the fantastic. This closed gastronomic circuit, a veritable culinary *machine célibataire,* was not unlike the inventions that grace Roussel's literary creations: isolated, eccentric, decadent, exquisite, narcissistic, phantasmatic, solipsistic, monomaniacal, insane. This anecdote reveals a veritable "locus solus" which poses a limit to the question of taste.

If a menu is to be read as a rhetorical and poetic exercise, then Roussel's taste was anything but exotic. He was, in fact, one of the last great patrons of the style of cuisine codified in Escoffier's *Le guide culinaire,* whose recipes were followed by Roussel's personal chef. Classic in his taste, Roussel was eccentric in his habits. Not unlike Ludwig II of Bavaria—who, having lost all political power and already beset by madness, touched by an infinite solitude, and haunted by incomparable phantasmagoria, spent only one day per year in his simulacra of Versailles constructed at Herrenchiensee, awaiting, before a table majestically set for two, the arrival of Louis XIV or Marie-Antoinette—Raymond Roussel would, in his mansion in Neuilly, dine alone, in total silence, condensing the three daily meals into a continuous service lasting from 12:30 to 5:30 in the afternoon. It is difficult not to assimilate the enigmatic (and now to us occasionally incomprehensible) names of these dishes with names in Roussel's novels; it is just as difficult not to note the anachronistic, decadent, precious, and excessive tone of the menu, both qualitatively and quantitatively. Such is the meal of a solipsist for whom food is everything . . . or nothing.

Colette, eightieth birthday dinner, hosted by the Académie Goncourt, composed by the Restaurant Drouant, held in her apartment in the Palais Royal, January 1953[18]

*Huîtres de Marennes*
*Coulibiac de Saumon à la Russe*
*Fricassée de Poulet au Champagne*
*Gâteau Quillet*

The logic of this menu is simple: it is composed of Colette's favorite dishes. An earlier celebration of this birthday—exulting the person whose writing on food was among the most sensual and perceptive ever—was hosted by Raymond Oliver at his restaurant Le Grand Véfour, at the foot of Colette's apartment, with the other guest of honor being Curnonsky. Colette requested a *Lièvre à la Royale "façon Colette,"* a hare cooked with forty cloves of garlic and forty shallots. As Oliver was unfamiliar with this recipe, he made both the desired dish and a more traditional version, a *Lièvre à la Royale garni de fois gras* (Hare garnished with foie gras).

Joseph Delteil, lunch, Monday[19]

*La soupe*

Delteil reminds us in *La cuisine paléolithique* that "One says soup like one says hare: it's that there is only one in the world." In this modern mythology of a primal cuisine—"Paleolithic cuisine is God's cuisine"—Delteil offers only fourteen recipes, "just for one week, but all the weeks of the world resemble each other, and here is a breviary for your entire life."[20] He knows of only three dishes (soup, fricassee, roast) and, as a symbol of culinary regional specificity, he especially revels in the specificity of the varied French patois "because it is closest to origins, richest in sperm, and most sacred."[21] Whatever one might think of this charming if conservative notion of cuisine and its ancient rootedness in the earth—what Delteil calls *cuisine brute*— this beloved book is certainly not without relation to the current culinary "ecologism" which is the latest mode, internationally expressed by the Slow Food movement.

Alain Senderens, L'Archestrate, 11 May 1979[22]

*Salade de Homard aux mangues et basilic*
*Saumon de la Loire au caviar*
*Émincé d'agneau à la crème d'ail*
*Plateau de fromages*
*Dessert de Grand-mère: Gâteau cassis, gâteau framboises, fraises des bois à l'ancienne*

The reason for the apperance of this menu is twofold: it is both exemplary of the nouvelle cuisine, and it represents the first meal of that genre I experienced. Readers are left to their own deductions.

Michel Bras, "Découverte & Nature" menu, Laguiole, 25 June 1995[23]

*Le gargouillou de jeunes légumes, relevé de graines germées et d'herbes champêtres*
*La lotte de Béganton pochée au beurre; une poêlée de girolles, de la peau de lait et du beurre "Noisette"*
*Le foie gras de canard poêlé & du choux "coeur de boeuf", de la ciboulette, du lard et de l'orange, étamines de Para*
*Des pois "sucre" dans une bouillon de leurs cosses; une crème aux truffes de pays*
*La poitrine de pigeon grillée, une pâte de citron au sel et de jeunes poireaux*
*Les fromages de Laguiole "vieux et jeune", des bleus et les fromages du marché*
*Le biscuit tiède de chocolat "coulant" aux arômes de cacao, sirop de sucre "noir" & "blond"*

*Dans une feuille de gentiane une compotée de pommes à la saveur amère, des baies de cassis et de groseilles roulées dans le sucre*
*Le croustillant de caramel et d'amandes, confit de cerises au serpolet d'ici*

The dishes of Michel Bras exemplify the complexity (in techniques, ingredients, inspirations) that characterizes the most successful contemporary cooking, effectively articulating the major dichotomies informing contemporary French cuisine—peasant / haute; traditional / nouvelle; simple / refined; wild / cultivated; raw / cooked—all the while stressing the primacy of the seasons and revealing the gustatory specificity of his region, the *goût du terroir.* It is indicative of his culinary complications that several of his dishes combine butter, oil, and animal fat: his restaurant in the Aubrac straddles the butter / olive oil line that roughly corresponds to France's watershed, separating "French" cuisine from its Provençal other; and is also not far from the goose and duck fat line, which demarcates Gascony and Languedoc from Provence. This inherent geo-culinary heterogeneity of basics is in itself an inspiration. Every border crossed or eliminated is to the benefit of cuisine.

Pierre Gagnaire, Paris, 16 December 1996[24]

*Beignets d'escargots accompagnés de petites tomates confites et d'un gnocci au vieux cantal*
*Ris de veau au grains de café*
*Homard en trois services : la gelée avec le corail, les pinces pochées, la queue rôtie*
*Des eaux glacées et du fromage blanc au safran, meringuage à l'italienne*

If I had to cite what I consider the cutting edge of contemporary European culinary art, I would probably top the list with Pierre Gagnaire. What might appear unpalatable in print is exquisite on the palate—such is the gastronomy of thresholds, the crux of innovation.

Jean-Georges Vongerichten, Vong, 16 August 1998

*Quail rubbed with Thai spices, crunchy cress salad*
*Spiced codfish with curried artichokes*
*Mango rice pudding, exotic fruit sorbet*

It is indicative of the international influences on Jean-Georges Vongerichten—an Alsatian who apprenticed in several great French restaurants, worked in Bangkok, Singapore, and London, and finally settled in New York—that his first book, *Simple Cuisine,* contains chapters entitled "On an Oriental Note" and (even more surprisingly, given the traditional French disdain for American cuisine) "An American Accent."[25] This is more than a polite bow to his adopted country, as both his ingredients and technical innovations are often decidedly ungallic, to the point that Vongerichten makes great use of local wild plants, notably herbs. (In one outing with friends in Connecticut, he discovered wood sorrel, garlic mustard, plantain greens, wild mint, spicebush berry, chickweed, and more; on another expedition in New York's Central Park, he found twenty-five species of edible plants growing wild.)[26] That branches of his restaurant Vong exist in New York, London, and Hong Kong is also a sign of this hybridization—polycultural if not quite postcolonial—as is a dish such as the *Shrimp salad, peppered melon, fig and sesame dressing,* yet another variant of the Vietnamese Shrimp and papaya salad already experimented upon by Senderens two decades ago (though Vongerichten's transformation is decidedly less Gallic).

The simultaneously operative—and apparently paradoxical—postmodern aesthetic conditions of regional singularity and multicultural melange have their culinary correlates in such contemporary "fusion cuisine." In a sense, every French cuisine throughout history has been "fusion" cuisine: court cuisine and haute cuisine have always assimilated products and techniques from both the French provinces and other countries. Yet it is a relatively recent phenomenon that such exotic products, presentations, and techniques have been valorized, symbolized, and showcased. Fusion can be experienced either as a mode of innovation or a threat of corruption, reviving age-old gastronomic debates. Though the centrifugal internationalism of Escoffier is, in the hands of chefs such as Bras, Gagnaire, Roellinger, Senderens, and Vongerichten, rapidly being replaced by a centripetal polyculturalism, the debate between tradition and innovation in French cuisine continues. The last great paradigm shift, contemporaneous with the aftermath of the events of May 1968, was the advent of the nouvelle cuisine—a reaction to the Escoffier style of haute cuisine that had dominated for nearly a century, in both France and all those countries influenced by its cuisine—established in the 1970s by Paul Bocuse, Georges Blanc, Alain Chapel, Michel Guérard, Paul Haeberlin, Gaston Lenôtre, Raymond Oliver, Jacques Pic, Alain Senderens, Jean and Pierre Troisgros, Roger Vergé, and championed by Henri Gault and Christian Millau, editors of the gastronomic guide bearing their names. In 1973 Gault and Millau published the ten commandments of the nouvelle cuisine:

> Thou shalt not overcook.
> Thou shalt utilize fresh products of high quality.
> Thou shalt lighten thy menu.
> Thou shalt not be systematically modernist.
> Thou shalt nevertheless seek what can be gained through new techniques.
> Thou shalt avoid marinades, hanging of game, fermentations, etc.
> Thou shalt eliminate brown and white sauces.
> Thou shalt not be oblivious to dietetics.
> Thou shalt not cheat on thy presentations.
> Thou shalt be inventive.[27]

The most recent variation on this theme is exemplified by the clash between two highly mediatized groups of French chefs, instigated in 1996 by the gastronomic journalist Marc Champérard (author of the food guide of the same name), who called for the safeguard of France's culinary "national identity," fustigating the "unbridled creativism" *(sic)* and "cosmopolitanism" of certain contemporary tendencies; he enlisted in his camp Joël Robuchon, Alain Ducasse, Georges Blanc, and Bernard Loiseau. (The use of the term *cosmopolitanism,* already evident in turn of the century debates about the "decadent" nature of haute cuisine, is certainly worthy of a major study.) The reaction was swift: Marc Veyrat organized the "Groupe des Huit" (group of eight)—Michel Bras, Jacques Chibois, Pierre Gagnaire, Jean-Michel Lorain, Alain Passard, Olivier Roellinger, Michel Troisgros, Marc Veyrat—linked by a manifesto:

> Claim our identity in a locale or a region, all the while respecting tradition.
> Valorize a modern cuisine of sensitivity and of new emotions.
> Be open to the world, and to professional and cultural exchange.
> Place oneself at the service of popular cuisine, which must again become the ambassador of our heritage.
> Revalorize the training of youth.[28]

It should be noted that while the dictates of the manifesto of the nouvelle cuisine were purely formal, those of the "Groupe des Huit" are psychological and sociological: in fact, both groups agree about the technical fundamentals of cooking, and the chefs of the nouvelle cuisine had always incorporated non-French products and techniques in order to create radically innovative (and thus nontraditional) dishes. The scission seems rather to be a generational one, between that oxymoron of a nouvelle classicism (first generation nouvelle cuisine chefs who, though open to the exotic, for the most part studied and worked primarily in France) and a second generation that often chooses lengthy stays abroad. The apparent rhetorical contradictions (or all-inclusiveness, depending on how one reads it) of the "Groupe des Huit" manifesto in fact indicates its particularly contemporary sensibility—regionalism / globalism; tradition / creativity; popular / haute; technical / emotional—precisely that mix of qualities previously considered incompatible, but now united in much of the most exciting French cuisine.

# Notes

*Preface*

1. Marcel Rouff, *La vie et la passion de Dodin-Bouffant, gourmet* (1924; Paris: Stock, 1984), 16. Unless otherwise noted, all translations are by the author.

2. Francesco Colonna, *Hypnerotomachia Poliphili* (Venice: Aldus Manutius, 1499); first French translation, *Discours du songe de Poliphile* (Paris: Kerver, 1546); first English translation, *The Strife of Love in a Dreame* (London: 1592); my translation is from the most recent French edition, transliterated and edited by Gilles Polizzi, *Le Songe de Poliphile* (Paris: Éditions de l'Imprimerie Nationale, 1994), 107–109; see Allen S. Weiss, *Unnatural Horizons: Paradox and Contradiction in Landscape Architecture* (New York: Princeton Architectural Press, 1998), 33–42.

3. André Félibien, *Relation de la fête de Versailles* (1668; Paris: Mercure de France, 1999), 12–13.

4. André Félibien, *Les Divertissements de Versailles* (1674), in *Les Fêtes de Versailles* (Paris: Éditions Dédale, Maisonneuve et Larose, 1994), 150–151. On fireworks, a much neglected art, see George Plimpton, *Fireworks: A History and Celebration* (New York: Doubleday, 1984).

5. See *Unnatural Horizons,* 109–117. By the end of the eighteenth century, the garden was recognized as a prime site for the excitation of all the senses, as expressed for example by the theorist of gardens C. C. L. Hirschfeld, in terms of the notion of "corresponding perceptions": "A grove decorated

with new foliage and agreeable distant vistas is all the more charming when at the same time we hear the song of the nightingale, the murmur of a waterfall, and we inhale the gentle odor of violettes." Cited in Alain Corbin, *Le miasme et la jonquille* (Paris: Flammarion / Champs, 1986), 95.

6. Cited in Jean-Louis Flandrin and Massimo Montanari, eds., *Histoire de l'alimentation* (Paris: Fayard, 1996), 700.

7. See Peter-Eckhard Knabe, "Esthétique et cuisine," in Jean-Claude Bonnet and Béatrice Fink, eds., *Aliments et cuisine,* a special issue of *Dix-Huitième Siècle* 15 (1983): 129–131. On late eighteenth-century transformations of cuisine, see Béatrice Fink, *Les liaisons savoureuses* (Saint-Étienne: Publications de l'Université de Saint-Étienne, 1995).

8. Alexandre Balthazar Laurent Grimod de la Reynière, *Écrits gastronomiques,* ed. Jean-Claude Bonnet (Paris: Union Générale d'Éditions, 1978).

9. Jean-Anthelme Brillat-Savarin, *Physiologie du goût* (1825; Paris: Flammarion, 1982), 251, 297.

10. James D. Carney, "The Style Theory of Art," *Pacific Philosophical Quarterly* 71, no. 4 (1991): 272–289.

11. Arthur Danto, "The Artworld," in J. Margolis, ed., *Philosophy Looks at the Arts* (Philadelphia: Temple University Press, 1987), 162.

12. Sung Bok Kim, "Is Fashion Art?", *Fashion Theory* 2, no. 1 (1998): 59.

13. Priscilla Parkhurst Ferguson, "A Cultural Field in the Making: Gastronomy in 19th-Century France," in Lawrence R. Schehr and Allen S. Weiss, eds., *French Food: On the Table, On the Page, and in French Culture* (New York: Routledge, 2001), 10.

14. Ibid., 601–602.

15. Ibid., 611–612.

16. Gaston Bachelard, *La psychanalyse du feu* (Paris: Gallimard, 1949), 38.

*Chapter 1. Drunken Space*

1. Jean-Claude Bonnet, "Introduction," in Grimod de la Reynière, *Écrits gastronomiques* (Paris: Union Générale d'Éditions, 1978), 30.

2. Ibid., 46.

3. Grimod de la Reynière, *Manuel des Amphitryons,* in *Écrits gastronomiques,* 382.

4. *Physiologie du goût,* 19.

5. Ibid., 170.

6. Roland Barthes, "Lecture de Brillat-Savarin" (1975), in *Oeuvres complètes,* Vol. 3 (Paris: Le Seuil, 1995), 293.

7. Ibid., 283.

8. Charles Baudelaire, "Du vin et du hachisch, comparés comme moyens de multiplication de l'individualité" (1851), in *Paradis artificiels* (1860), in *Oeuvres complètes,* Vol. 1 (Paris: Gallimard / Pléiade, 1975), 378. On the issue of intoxication from the point of view of the sense of smell, see "L'ivresse et le flacon," in *Le miasme et la jonquille,* 235–246. In a very different context, also of interest is Wolfgang Schivelbusch, *Tastes of Paradise: A Social History of Spices, Stimulants, and Intoxicants* (New York: Vintage,1993).

9. "Lecture de Brillat-Savarin," 282–283.

10. *Paradis artificiels,* 379.

11. Ibid., 381.

12. Ibid., 383. It should be noted that the earliest examples of the sublime, notably those of Burke and Kant, consisted of the experience of the most terrifying aspects of the landscape; to date, the concept of the sublime has hardly been considered in terms of cuisine.

13. Charles Baudelaire, "Hymne à la beauté" (1860), *Les fleurs du mal,* in *Ouevres complètes,* Vol. 1, 25.

14. *Paradis artificiels,* 397.

15. Ibid., 409.

16. Ibid., 426. The polemic of a "man-god" is central to

Nietzsche's Zarathustra, though as a positive principle, determined by a Dionysian notion of intoxication.

17. Ibid., 440.

18. Ibid., 392.

19. Ibid., 431.

20. Ibid., 378.

21. Charles Baudelaire, letter to Richard Wagner, 17 February 1860, in *L'art Romantique* (Paris: Flammarion, 1968), 264.

22. Charles Baudelaire, "Richard Wagner et *Tannhäuser* à Paris," in *L'art Romantique,* 270.

23. Ibid., 273.

24. Ibid., 271.

25. Ibid., 272.

26. Ibid., 292.

27. For a study of Baudelarian temporality, see Georges Poulet, *Études sur le temps humain,* Vol. 1 (1952; Paris: Éditions du Rocher, 1989), 364–385.

28. "Richard Wagner et *Tannhäuser* à Paris," 281.

29. Ibid., 281.

30. Gaston Bachelard, *La terre et les rêveries du repos* (Paris: José Corti, 1948), 81.

31. Ibid., 82.

32. Ibid., 85.

33. See Allen S. Weiss, "Erotic Nostalgia and the Inscription of Desire," in Allen S. Weiss, ed., *Experimental Sound and Radio* (Cambridge: MIT Press, 2001), 8–21. This problematic was at the core of Arthur Schopenhauer's *The World as Will and Idea,* which had a profound influence on Nietzsche.

34. Jonathan Crary, *Techniques of the Observer* (Cambridge: MIT Press, 1992), 91.

35. Charles Baudelaire, letter of 21 January 1856 to Toussenel, in *Oeuvres complètes,* Vol. 1, 841.

36. *Techniques of the Observer,* 93.

37. See Michel Foucault, "Fantasia of the Library" (1967), in *Language, Counter-Memory, Practice,* trans. Donald F.

Bouchard and Sherry Simon (Ithaca: Cornell University Press, 1977), 87–109, where Foucault argues that Gustave Flaubert's *La tentation de Saint Antoine* is the first modernist novel, since its origin was not derived from sheer poetic intuition, but rather from a compendium of diverse works researched in the archive. For the genealogy of the "anatomy" as a hybrid literary genre—which includes works such as The Bible, Francesco Colonna's *Hypnerotomachia Poliphili,* Robert Burton's *Anatomy of Melancholy,* James Joyce's *Finnegans Wake,* Antonin Artaud's *The Umbilicus of Limbo*—see Allen S. Weiss, "An Anatomy of Anatomy," *The Drama Review* 162 (1999).

38. Cited in Romi, *Histoire des festins insolites et de la goinfrerie* (Paris: Éditions Artulen, 1993), 153.

39. Cited in Joanna Richardson, *Baudelaire* (London: John Murray, 1994), 348.

40. Arthur Rimbaud, letter of 13 May 1871 to Georges Izambard, in *Poésies, Une saison en enfer, Illuminations* (Paris: Gallimard / Poésies, 1984), 200.

41. Friedrich Nietzsche, *The Birth of Tragedy* (1872), trans. Walter Kaufman (New York: Vintage, 1967), 33. See David B. Allison, "Nietzsche's 'On Music and Words'," *New Nietzsche Studies* (Fall 1996): 15–41.

42. *The Birth of Tragedy,* 40.

43. Ibid., 46.

44. Friedrich Nietzsche, *Twilight of the Idols* (1888), in *The Portable Nietzsche,* trans. Walter Kaufmann (New York: Penguin, 1980), 518. It must not be forgotten that the myth of Dionysus culminates in a murderous sacrifical feast. The historical literature on Dionysian rites is vast; to cite just a few major works: Maria Daraki, *Dionysos* (Paris: Arthaud, 1985); Marcel Detienne, *Dionysos Slain* (Baltimore: Johns Hopkins University Press, 1979); Marcel Detienne, *Dionysos à ciel ouvert* (Paris: Hachette, 1986); Walter F. Otto, *Dionysus: Myth and Cult* (1933; Bloomington: Indiana University Press, 1965). Nietzsche occasionally comments on the metaphysics of cuisine, though usually subsumed in the context of a greater anat-

omy: "Whatever proceeds from the stomach, the intestines, the beating of the heart, the nerves, the bile, the semen—all those distempers, debilitations, excitations, the whole chance operation of the machine of which we still know so little!—had to be seen by a Christian such as Pascal as a moral and religious phenomenon, and he had to ask whether God or Devil, good or evil, salvation or damnation, was to be discovered in them! Oh what an unhappy interpreter!" (*Daybreak,* ¶86). See the brilliant analysis of these issues in David B. Allison, *Reading the New Nietzsche* (Lanham, MD: Rowman & Littlefield, 2001).

45. Friedrich Nietzsche, *Thus Spoke Zarathustra* (1885), in *The Portable Nietzsche,* 251–253 (this passage is condensed for the sake of brevity).

46. Theodor Adorno, *In Search of Wagner* (1952; London, Verso, 1985), 87. See Annette Michelson, "Bayreuth: The Centennial *Ring,*" *October* 14 (1980): 65–70.

47. *In Search of Wagner,* 86.

48. *Thus Spoke Zarathustra,* 435.

49. Charles Baudelaire, *Petits poèmes en prose,* in *Paradis artificiels* (Paris: Flammarion, 1966), 188. One might note that Huysmans, in *À rebours* (1884; Paris: Gallimard Folio, 1977), 320, claims that "[i]n a word, the prose poem represented, for des Esseintes, the concrete juice, the *osmazôme* of literature, the essential oil of art." For the other side of the matter, see for example the culinary considerations in one of Baudelaire's prose works, *La Fanfarlo* (1847), in *Oeuvres complètes,* Vol. I. Baudelaire's actual appreciation of food and wine greatly surpassed his poetic evocations of their pleasures.

50. Cited in *Études sur le temps humains,* Vol. I, 368.

51. See Marcel Detienne, *Dionysos à ciel ouvert,* 42; and Allen S. Weiss, "Possession Trance and Dramatic Perversity," in *The Aesthetics of Excess* (Albany: State University of New York Press, 1989), 3–11.

52. Cited in Gilbert Garrier, *Histoire sociale et culturelle du vin* (Paris: Bordas, 1996), 275. Our contemporary versions of this device would be the digital counters of blood alcohol con-

tent being proposed for use in American bars, or the dreaded balloons used by the police in DWI tests. It is interesting to note that many metiers established metaphors about drunkenness specific to their own usages; for example (one that need be cited in French), in musicians' slang of the nineteenth century, "un ivrogne est un '*fa* bémol' parce qu'il vomit ('vaut *mi*'!); s'il tombe, il est un '*fa* dièse,' parce qu'il est 'près du *sol*'" (277). It would not be totally amiss to consider Artaud's state of the "body without organs," a condition intimately linked to intoxication and its cures, in relation to the last degree of drunkenness, "plein comme un oeuf," indicated on the "Thermomètre du Pochard."

53. Honoré de Balzac, "Traité des excitants modernes" (1839), in *Oeuvres diverses,* Vol. 3 (Paris: Louis Conard Libraire-Éditeur, 1940), 183.

54. Ibid., 184.

55. The epistemic shift of the nineteenth century included a vast medicalization of theological phenomena. One might consider, in this context, the history of the possessed women of Morzine, a town in Haute Savoie, which began in 1857 (the year of the trail of *Les fleurs du mal*), only to end sixteen years later. This case of demoniacal possession (one largely suppressed in the annals of medical history), was the first in France in which the determination of the cause of the demoniacal/hysterical disturbance was imposed by the medical and political establishment, rather than the Church. See Allen S. Weiss, "The Theater of Possession," *Sulfur* 33 (1993): 134–136.

56. Paul-Émile Littré, *Dictionnaire de la langue française,* Vol. 2 (Monte-Carlo: Éditions du Cap, 1974), 3320.

57. The notion of aesthesiology was most fully developed in Maurice Merleau-Ponty, *Phenomenology of Perception,* trans. Colin Smith (1945; London: Routledge & Kegan Paul, 1962).

58. Charles Baudelaire, *Fusées* (1862), in *Oeuvres Complètes,* Vol. I, 649.

59. Grimod de la Reynière, *Almanach des gourmands,* Vol.

2 (Paris: 1804), 73–74; cited in the introduction to *Écrits gastronomiques,* 68–69. The shop of Monsieur Dutfoy was to be found on 233, rue de l'Arbre-sec. This occurance of the *pièce montée* presented as a dramatic scene is hardly unique. See, for example, the scene of the great nineteenth-century Polish feast in Adam Mickiewicz's *Pan Tadeusz,* where the heat of the room wreaks havoc with the fragile pastry creation, adorned by a *pièce montée* reproducing a Polish village scene:

> The centerpiece, like a star that will not swerve,
> From its appointed path, was changing season,
> The golden grain slowly melted,
> Warmed by thermal treason.

60. Antonin Carême, "Avertissement," *Le Pâtissier Pittoresque* (Paris: 1815). For more detail on Carême's *pièces montées,* see Jean-Claude Bonnet, "Carême, or the Last Sparks of Decorative Cuisine," trans. Sophie Hawkes, in Allen S. Weiss, ed., *Taste Nostalgia* (New York: Lusitania Press, 1997), 155–182; Georges Bernier, *Antonin Carême* (Paris: Grasset, 1989); and the exhibition catalogue, *Antonin Carême: L'Art culinaire au XIXe siècle* (Paris: Orangerie de Bagatelle, 1984).

61. *La terre et les rêveries du repos,* 80.

*Chapter 2. The Ideology of the Pot-au-feu*

1. Cited in Romi, *Histoire des festins insolites et de la goinfrerie,* 87. See the issue of *Autrement* (Paris: 1999) dedicated to the pot-au-feu.

2. Claude Lévi-Strauss, *L'origine des manières de table* (Paris: Plon, 1968), 397. This is an expansion of his analysis first made explicit in *Le cru et le cuit* (The Raw and the Cooked) Paris: Plon, 1964).

3. Ibid., 400.

4. Ibid., 401. See also Claude Fischler, *L'Homnivore* (Paris: Éditions Odile Jacob, 1990), 46.

5. *L'origine des manières de table,* 402. One might note, in the specifically French context, the literary value of these observations. In Balzac's *Le Cousin Pons,* for example, when the inveterate gourmet Pons falls ill, his landlady prepares a pot-au-feu to help bring him back to health. Honoré de Balzac, *Le Cousin Pons* (1847; Paris: Gallimard / Folio, 1973), 314.

6. *L'origine des manières de table,* 402.

7. Ibid., 403.

8. Antonin Carême, *L'art de la cuisine française au XIXe siècle* (1832; Paris: Éditions Payot et Rivages, 1994), 23.

9. Ibid., 23–24.

10. Roland Barthes, "Lecture de Brillat-Savarin," 288.

11. *Physiologie du goût,* 81–82.

12. Among the numerous reissues and translations of this classic among classics, the English-speaking reader can consult Auguste Escoffier, *The Escoffier Cookbook* (New York: Crown Publishers 1969). In his autobiography, Escoffier admits to having once served a pot-au-feu upon the special request of a client. While it is true that Alexandre Dumas's *Le Grand dictionnaire de cuisine* (Paris: 1873) and *Petit dictionnaire de cuisine* (1882) both contain an entry on the pot-au-feu, the information consists mainly of material recycled from other authors, and thus hardly constitutes a living testimony to the pot-au-feu in its contemporary moment. Furthermore, at the end of the entry, he manages to assimilate the pot-au-feu to cabbage soup!

13. Joris-Karl Huysmans, *Là-bas* (1891; Paris: Gallimard / Folio, 1985), back cover; this edition was established and prefaced by Yves Hersant. Romi, in *Histoire des festins insolites et de la goinfrerie,* 87, recounts the words of an English preacher at the end of the eighteenth century: "The POT is the Church, the MEAT is the Word of God . . . the BOUILLON, grace from Above and the THREE FEET OF THE KETTLE are the symbol of the Trinity!" For a particularly humorous blasphemy on the theme, see Michel Maxence, "Les amateurs d'hosties," *Tel Quel* 9 (1962).

14. *La-bàs,* 84.

15. Ibid., 84–85.

16. Ibid., 85–86.

17. Ibid., 89.

18. Note that in Balzac's *Le Cousin Pons,* the dish offered Pons is referred to as a "sacramental pot-au-feu."

19. *La-bàs,* 342. On the restorative powers of bouillon and its relation to the birth of the restaurant, see Rebecca L. Spang's exhaustive *The Invention of the Restaurant: Paris and Modern Gastronomic Culture.* (Cambridge, MA: Harvard University Press, 2000), 12–63.

20. Marcel Rouff, *La vie et la passion de Dodin-Bouffant, gourmet,* 83–7.

21. Lawrence R. Schehr, "Savory Writing: Marcel Rouff's *Vie et passion de Dodin-Bouffant,*" in Schehr and Weiss, eds., *French Food,* 132–133.

22. *Dodin-Bouffant,* 97. The menu begins with a *platter of hors-d'oeuvres,* including chanterelles and crayfish in aspic, small trout stuffed with tarragon and chopped olives, Payerne sausages, creamed hashed pidgeon, forcemeat stuffed eggs, roasts covered with mashed duck liver, cheese croquettes, cold deboned thrush, anchovies, soft-roe filled pastry shells flavored with cloves and red pepper, lemoned tuna, cold eels stuffed with shrimp purée, game sausages, and fresh butter; it is followed by a *soup* consisting of a strong double consommé of beef and vegetables to which was added a cream of mushrooms and white asparagus, chicken stock, and egg whites beaten with nutmeg; the soup was garnished with artichoke bottoms stuffed with a filling made of carp soft-roe, mushrooms, and cream, as well as cheese and crayfish croquettes; afterward is a dish of *assorted fritters,* variously containing monkfish liver, safronned marrow, marinaded woodcock brains, cardoons; then came the famous *pot-au-feu,* followed by an *onion purée,* and completed with an unnamed *dessert.*

23. Ibid., 103.

24. Ibid., 104–105. As extravagent and unrealistically complex as this dish might seem today, it is in fact parallel, in

difficulty, style and cost, to a mode of haute bourgeoise cuisine that has been given relatively little note in the history of gastronomy, that of cooking after the hunt. In the lineage of our present study, see, for example, the unjustly forgotten book by Lucien Tendret, *La Table au pays de Brillat-Savarin* (Belley: Bailley, 1892). Here Tendret, nephew of the famed gastronome, Brillat-Savarin, describes a dish, offered by Monseigneur Gabriel Cortois de Quinsey, Bishop of Belley, to his canons for the feast of Notre-Dame, consisting of pastry crust lined with a forcemeat (containing chopped veal and pork flesh, chicken livers, black truffles, egg, and cognac), upon which are placed the marinated parts of numerous gamebirds (greenshank, snipe, quail, partridge, corncrake, and whole beccafico, to which are added cockscombs, mushrooms, black truffles, and butter), all topped off with another layer of forcemeat, and sealed with a pastry crust perforated in the center. A sauce is prepared by crushing the birds' entrails and stomachs, moistened with beef bouillon, marinade, and white wine, all of which is reduced and then strained, to be added to the pie before serving. Try and imagine what such a dish would cost in a restaurant today, when a single snipe or woodcock is an extreme luxury, the rare times one is even available. Furthermore, how many of us would actually enjoy the intense, and decidedly high and fecal, flavors of this dish? Indeed, one of the forgotten cuisines—with its own codes of ostentation—is that of the hunt, once at the summit of aristocratic passions, and now relegated to a small subculture. Rare is the restaurant that does total justice to game. (One might note that the hunt has become a political and moral issue in France, especially in the region surrounding Bordeaux, where hunters have recently made the illegal shooting of thrush a *cause célèbre.*)

25. *Dodin-Bouffant,* 108.

26. See Alberto Capatti, "La croisade des régionalistes," in *Le goût du nouveau* (Paris: Alban Michel, 1989), 223–225.

27. Cited in Adam Gopnik, "Is There a Crisis in French Cooking?," *The New Yorker* (April 28 & May 5, 1997), 154.

28. *Le goût du nouveau,* 232.

29. Dumaine's restaurant is of particular historic importance, since it was one of the principal gastronomic stops on the way from Paris to the South before the construction of the *autoroute* (express highway). It was, therefore, for the several decades he practiced, a major nexus of the intersection of regional and haute cuisine. Bernard Loiseau, who now owns this restaurant, maintains the same tradition.

Details about this menu come from articles displayed in the old dining room (now a small culinary museum) of the Hôtel de la Côte d'Or. The four services of the pot-au-feu are as follows: 1. the sausage with truffles and pistachios is served with steamed potatoes and fresh butter; 2. the ham with a Soubise sauce; 3. the chicken with a mousseline of foie gras; 4. the rump steak with boiled vegetables, accompanied with truffled forcemeats, hearts of celery, and artichoke bottoms.

Robert Courtine reports four other instances where, in one manner or another, the pot-au-feu of Dodin-Bouffant was realized (all, coincidentally, in Paris): twice at the restaurant Prunier; once by Jacques Manière at his restaurant, Le Pactole; and once, in a rather bizarre version by Raymond Oliver, a *pot-au-feu en vessie,* that is, cooked in a pig's bladder! Cited in, "Un précieux témoignage de Robert Courtine," in Françoise Colin, *Et Marcel Rouff créa Dodin-Bouffant* (Dijon: Darantiere, 1988), 135.

30. Of course, the very meaning of the dish, pot-au-feu, suggests an open and generic usage, thus many dishes are named "pot-au-feu" by analogy; an extreme example is the "Perroquet en pot-au-feu" described by Docteur André Nègre in *Antilles et Guyane à travers leur cuisine* (Paris: Éditions Caribéennes, 1985), 123.

*Chapter 3. In the Devil's Kitchen*

1. Michel Carrouges, "Mode d'emploi," in Jean Clair and Harald Szeeman, *Junggesellenmaschinen / Les Machines*

*Célibataires* (Venice: Alfieri, 1975), 21. See also Michel Carrouges, *Les machines célibataires* (Paris: Arcanes, 1954); Jean Clair, ed., *L'Ame au corps* (Paris: Réunion des Musées Nationaux / Gallimard / Electa, 1993); and Alberto Capatti, *Le goût du nouveau,* 33–60.

2. These negative limits of the culinary field contain phenomena such as anorexia, aphrodisiacs, ascetic renunciation, black magic potions, white magic elixirs, bulemia, cannibalism, coprophagy, junkfood, erotic philtres, spiritual macrobiotics, neurotic oral fixations, poisons, religious prohibitions, psychotic deliria. I have chosen a small but symbolically rich part of this field for my study. I have elsewhere examined the psycholinguistic relations between speech and excretion, that is, between the two extremes of the digestive tract, mouth and anus, a symbolic axis at the core of Artaud's rhetoric and poetics; see "From Schizophrenia to Schizophonica," in *Phantasmic Radio* (Durham, NC, Duke University Press, 1995), 9–34; on Artaud's glossolalia, see Allen S. Weiss, "Psychopompomania," in *The Aesthetics of Excess,* 113–134. The locus classicus on the subject is Mikhail Bakhtin, *Rabelais and His World,* trans. Hélène Iswolsky (1965; Cambridge, MA: MIT Press, 1968).

3. M. F. K. Fisher, *An Alphabet for Gourmets* (1940), reprinted in *The Art of Eating* (New York: Vintage Books, 1976), 601.

4. Grimod de la Reynière, *Itinéraire nutritif ou Promenade d'un gourmand dans divers quartiers de Paris* (1803; Paris: Union Générale d'Éditions, 1978), 282.

5. "Etude psychologique et analyse phénoménologique d'un cas de mélancolie schizophrénique," *Journal de Psychologie* (Paris: 1923), 6; cited in Eugène Minkowski, *Lived Time,* trans. Nancy Metzel (Evanston: Northwestern University Press, 1970), 180–181.

6. Jean Genet, *Notre-Dame-des-Fleurs* (1948; Paris: Gallimard / Folio,1996), 43.

7. Jean Genet, *Pompes funèbres* (1953; Paris: Gallimard /

L'Imaginaire, 1978), 27. This perverse gesture of love may be compared to parallel expressions of suspicion, hatred, and ideological loathing. Victor Hugo, in *Les travailleurs de la mer,* recounts the following: "The judicious and wise king James I had that sort of woman boiled alive, tasted the bouillon, and, according to its taste, said: *She was a sorceress,* or: *She wasn't one."* (1866; Paris: GF-Flammarion, 1980; 125.) Such is a terrifying and terroristic use of the pot-au-feu.

8. Antonin Artaud, *Héliogabale ou l'anarchiste couronné* (1934), in *Oeuvres complètes* (Paris: Gallimard, 1982), 39. On the symbolism of blood, see Piero Camporesi, *Juice of Life: The Symbolic and Magic Significance of Blood,* trans. Robert R. Barr (1988; New York: Continuum, 1995). "To write with one's blood" is perhaps the most poignant, if most clichéd, metaphor for literary truth.

9. Jean-Pierre Vernant, "Introduction," in Marcel Detienne, *Les jardins d'Adonis* (Paris: Gallimard, 1972), xxxiii. Needless to say, all structuralist considerations of cuisine must refer to the four monumental volumes of Claude Lévi-Strauss's *Mythologiques* (Paris: Plon, 1964–1971).

10. Antonin Artaud, *Correspondance avec Jacques Rivière* (1924), in *Oeuvres complètes,* Vol. I, Part 1 (Paris: Gallimard, 1984), 43.

11. Antonin Artaud, "Le rite du peyotl chez les Tarahumaras" (1943), *Les Tarahumaras,* in *Oeuvres complètes,* Vol. IX (Paris: Gallimard, 1971), 37. Note that *Les Tarahumaras* consists of a heterogeneous collection of writings begun in 1936 ("La Montagne des Signes"), with several texts written during his incarceration at Rodez (notably the 1943 "Le Rite du Peyotl chez les Tarahumaras"), and the last text, "Tutuguri," having been written just before his death in February 1948. The version of "Tutuguri" that appears in *Les Tarahumaras* is the second of two, the first being part of the radiophonic work, *Pour en finir avec le jugement de dieu* (1948).

12. Antonin Artaud, *Le théâtre et son double* (1938), in *Oeuvres complètes,* Vol. IV (Paris: Gallimard, 1964), 18.

13. Antonin Artaud, *Messages révolutionaires* (1936), in *Oeuvres complètes,* Vol. VIII (Paris: Gallimard, 1971), 269.

14. Antonin Artaud, "Notes sur les cultures orientales" (1935), in *Oeuvres complètes,* Vol. VIII, 164.

15. Antonin Artaud, *Fragments d'un journal d'enfer* (1926), in *Oeuvres complètes,* Vol. I, Part 1, 117.

16. Antonin Artaud, "La danse du peyotl," in *Les Tarahumaras,* in *Oeuvres complètes,* Vol. IX, 62; see also "L'Évêque de Rodez," in *Oeuvres complètes,* Vol. IX, 219.

17. Ibid., 50.

18. Antonin Artaud, letter of 4 February 1937 to Jean Paulhan, in *Oeuvres complètes,* Vol. IX, 125.

19. *Héliogabale,* 14.

20. "Le rite du peyotl chez les Tarahumaras," 24.

21. Antonin Artaud, "Tutuguri" (1947), in *Oeuvres complètes,* Vol. IX, 69.

22. On the question of infinity in Artaud, see Camille Dumoulié, *Antonin Artaud* (Paris: Le Seuil, 1996), 142–148.

23. "Tutuguri," 27.

24. "La danse du peyotl," 62.

25. Antonin Artaud, *Ci-Gît* (1948), in *Oeuvres complètes,* Vol. XII (Paris: Gallimard, 1974), 90–91. The translation used is from Antonin Artaud, *"Here-Lies,"* in *Watchfiends & Rack-screams: Works from the Final Period of Antonin Artaud,* trans. Clayton Eshleman with Bernard Bador (Boston: Exact Change, 1995), 219–220. One might note that such an omelette would have the taste of bitter almonds and capers, which for Artaud would have evoked childhood memories of Marseilles and Mediterranean cuisine. In one of his many moments of dark humor, Artaud writes, in regard to the great esoteric and alchemical tradition: "Yes indeed, the great work and the *poule au pot* [boiled chicken] are adjacent in certain minds" (*Oeuvres complètes,* Vol. XXIII, 206).

26. Dumoulié, *Antonin Artaud,* 122.

27. Antonin Artaud, letter of 22 September 1945 to Henri Parisot, in *Oeuvres complètes,* Vol. IX, 186.

28. Gilles Deleuze and Félix Guattari, *Milles plateaux* (Paris: Minuit, 1980), 189–190. Deleuze and Guattari's earlier work, *L'anti-oedipe* (Paris: Minuit, 1972), utilized Artaud's enunciation of the body without organs as its major anti-metaphysical and anti-psychoanalytic term.

29. Antonin Artaud, Post-Scriptum, dated 23 March 1947, to "Le rite du peyotl chez les Tarahumaras," 40–41. For a more detailed analysis, see Allen S. Weiss, "Libidinal Mannerisms and Profligate Abominations," in Edward Scheer, ed., *100 Years of Cruelty: Essays on Artaud* (Sydney: Power Publications and Artspace, 2000), 103–129.

*Chapter 4. The Epic of the Cephalopod*

1. Victor Hugo, *Les travailleurs de la mer* (1866), in *Oeuvres complètes,* Roman III (Paris: Laffont / Bouquins, 1985), 279; for an illustration of this drawing, see Roger Pierrot and Judith Petit, eds., *Soleil d'encre : Manuscrits et dessins de Victor Hugo* (Paris: Éditions Paris Musées / Bibliothèque Nationale, 1985), 216.

2. *Les travailleurs de la mer,* 181.

3. Laurent Jenny, *La terreur et les signes : Poétiques de rupture* (Paris: Gallimard, 1982), 107.

4. *Les travailleurs de la mer,* 278.

5. Cited in Roger Caillois, *La pieuvre : Essai sur la logique de l'imaginaire* (Paris: La Table Ronde, 1973), 89. Caillois's book is an excellent source for the factual history of the squid, in the context of its literary transformations. One of the rare humoristic moments in this history occurred when in 1996 National Public Radio offered a report of a giant squid sighted off New Zealand, followed by a comical interview with the fictional Chef Guillaume, asking how he would cook and serve such a creature.

6. Cited in *La Pieuvre,* 75.

7. Maryline Desbiolles, *La seiche* (Paris: Le Seuil, 1998), 19. All translations are my own. An English translation of this

book appeared as *The Cuttlefish,* trans. Mara Bertelsen (New York: Herodias, 2001).

8. It might well be noted that in several instances, the great repository and stylist of Gallic memory, Marcel Proust, celebrated the qualities of Pampille's culinary writing in *À la recherche du temps perdu.*

9. This paragraph reunites the twelve chapter titles into the original recipe.

10. It was here that I ate the most surreal dish I ever experienced, a *risotto de fruits de mer* topped with dried bonito shavings: the heat of the dish caused the extremely thin bonito flakes to rise and undulate, a miniature scene worthy of the culinary imagination of a Dali or a Tanguy.

11. *La seiche,* 105.

12. Ibid., 12.

13. Ibid., 48.

14. Ibid., 45.

15. Ibid., 48. For another reading of white food of childhood, see Chantal Thomas, "Blancmange with Almond Milk," in *Taste, Nostalgia,* 17–19.

16. *La Seiche,* 48.

17. Ibid., 7.

18. Ibid., 7.

19. Ibid., 88.

20. Ibid., 85.

21. Ibid., 52.

22. *Physiologie du goût,* 111.

23. Antonin Artaud, "Correspondance de la momie" (1927), in *Oeuvres complètes,* Vol. I, Part II (Paris: Gallimard, 1976), 57.

24. *Les travailleurs de la mer,* 285.

25. *La seiche,* 52.

26. Ibid., 27.

27. Ibid., 11.

28. Ibid., 90.

29. François Rabelais, *Le Tiers livre* (1546), in *Oeuvres*

*complètes* (Paris: Le Seuil, 1973), 367. The fact that the conjugation of the word *rire* (laugh) in the old orthography gives the term *riz* (rice) is a charming coincidence in this context.

30. *La seiche,* 58.
31. *Les travailleurs de la mer,* 283.
32. *La seiche,* 25–26.
33. Ibid., 103.
34. Ibid., 62.
35. Ibid., 70.
36. Ibid., 118.
37. D. A. F. Sade, *La Philosophie dans le boudoir* (1795), in *Oeuvres complètes,* Vol. XXV (Paris: Éditions Jean-Jacques Pauvert, 1968), 312. See Allen S. Weiss, "A New History of the Passions," in *The Aesthetics of Excess,* 43–53.
38. *La seiche,* 122.
39. Ibid., 90.

*Chapter 5. Tractatus Logico-Gastronomicus*

1. Émile Littré, *Dictionnaire de la langue française,* Vol. 2 (Monte-Carlo: Éditions du Cap, 1974), 2814.
2. Cultural studies has motivated vast amounts of writing on fastfood and junkfood conceived as a major sociological phenomenon; they are occasionally also considered in culinary terms, either as a counter-ideal opposed to the heights of "transcendental" cuisine, or as a means to argue for the total subjectivization or nonhierarchization of culinary values. However—while usually avoiding polemic on these matters, since they originate in a very different, indeed antithetical universe of values from my own—I still await the word of a great chef who claims any inspiration whatsoever from such food. Furthermore, in response to criticisms of hierarchical aesthetic judgments, quite frankly, I have never yet heard anybody say, "Hey, let's go out for an awful meal." The notion of "taste," when practically utilized in regard to food, almost always implies good taste. I wish to insist that this position is not at all a

manifestation of culinary snobbism, since the very poorest of peasant foods—in fact much less expensive, more nourishing, and simpler than fastfood, and still as ubiquitous and widely appreciated—have inspired haute cuisine from its inception. Consider onion soup, cabbage soup, and that Provençal garlic soup whose name so poetically indicates a zero-degree of the culinary arts, *aïgo bouïllido,* "boiled water."

3. Marcel Proust, *Du côté de chez Swann* (1913; Paris: Gallimard, 1987), 70. For discussions of post-childhood influences on the formation of taste, see Claude Fischler, *L'homnivore,* and John Thorne with Matt Lewis Thorne, *Outlaw Cook* (New York: Farrar, Straus, Giroux, 1992).

4. Philippe Gillet, *Le goût et les mots: Littérature et gastronomie (XIVe–XXe siècles)* (Paris: Payot, 1993), 104.

5. Jean-François Revel, *La sensibilité gastronomique de l'Antiquité à nos jours* (Paris: Éditions Suger, 1985), 21.

6. See Umberto Eco, "How Culture Conditions the Colors We See," in Marshall Blonsky, *On Signs* (Baltimore: Johns Hopkins University Press, 1985), 157–175.

7. See Martine Chatelain-Courtois, *Les mots du vin et de l'ivresse* (Paris: Belin, 1984).

8. Jean Dubuffet, "Un grand salut très différent au Martelandre," in *Écrits bruts,* ed. Michel Thévoz (Paris: Presses Universitaires de France, 1979), 231.

9. Michel Serres, *Les cinq sens* (Paris: Hachette, 1985), 206.

10. *L'homnivore,* 264.

11. Ibid., 263.

*Postface*

1. Philippe Gillet, *Le goût et les mots,* 5. Note that the translation of all dishes on the menus cited in this postface would be impossible, given the fact that the names of many classic French dishes are codes to indicate complex recipes and sauces. To the contrary, contemporary menus often indicate

dishes not by name but in terms of ingredients and techniques. When feasible, translations will be provided in the notes.

2. Joris-Karl Huysmans, *À rebours,* 90 and 392, note 16. See also Grimod de la Reynière, *Écrits gastronomiques,* 16–17 and 405–418. [Tortoise soup; Russian rye bread; Turkish olives; caviar; pressed mullet roe; Frankfurt sausages; game in licorice colored sauce; truffle coulis; ambered chocolate cream; pudding; nectarines, grapes, blackberries, cherries.]

3. D. A. F. Sade, *Oeuvres complètes* Vol. XIII (Paris: Pauvert, 1966), 46–47. Note that Sade addresses one famous letter to his wife in strange terms of endearment: "Porc frais de ma pensée" (fresh pork of my thought). On Sadian cuisine, see Béatrice Fink, "Lecture alimentaire de l'utopie sadienne," in Michel Camus and Philippe Roger, eds., *Sade, écrire la crise* (Paris: Belfond, 1983), 175–191; Béatrice Bomel-Rainelli, "Sade ou l'alimentation générale," in *Aliments et cuisine,* 199–210. On aphrodisiacs in the eighteenth century, see Lydia Vázquez, "Ratafia and Other Love Potions," in *Taste, Nostalgia,* 79–88. [Bouillon made from twenty-four sparrows with rice and saffron; pie with meatballs of hashed pigeon garnished with artichoke bottoms; vanilla cream; truffles Provençal; turkey garnished with truffles; eggs in gravy; hash of partridge breast stuffed with truffles and fortified wine; Champagne; ambergris compote.]

4. For the full menu, see Jean-Paul Aron, *Le mangeur au XIXe siècle* (1973; Paris: Denoël/Gonthier, 1976), 34–38.

5. Georges Bernier, *Antonin Carême,* 217.

6. *Histoire des festins insolites et de la goinfrerie,* 133. The source of this information is Edmond Werdet, *Portrait intime de Balzac* (Paris: E. Dentu, 1879). Food was a crucial element of Balzac's fiction; see, for example, *Le ventre de Paris* and *Le cousin Pons.* [Hors-d'oeuvres; 100 Ostende oysters; 12 veal cutlets; a duck with turnips; two roast partridges; sole à la normande; fruit; a pear dessert.]

7. Robert Courtine, *Feasts of a Militant Gastronome,* trans. June Guicharnaud (New York: William Morrow & Co.,

1974), 18. This menu is on display in the private museum of La Tour d'Argent in Paris: which is lined with paneling from one of the salons of the Café Anglais.

8. Ibid., 181. On culinary exoticism in the French context, see *Le goût du nouveau,* 187–212. [Stuffed head of donkey; elephant consommé; roast camel; kangaroo stew; roast bear cutlets in pepper sauce; haunch of wolf in roe-deer sauce; cat surrounded by rats; truffled antelope terrine. Note the suggestive pairings of biological enemies: cat / rat and wolf / deer.]

9. On the formation of taste, see *L'Homnivore;* for an exemplary study of the political implications of culinary abjection, see Doris Witt, "Soul Food: Where the Chitterling Hits the [Primal] Pan," in Ron Scapp and Brian Seitz, eds., *Eating Culture* (Albany: State University of New York Press, 1998), 258–287.

10. Stéphane Mallarmé, *La dernière mode,* in *Oeuvres complètes* (Paris: Gallimard/Pléiade, 1945), 735–136. [Salted herrings; country sausage; fresh butter; terrine of young hare; cold partridges in aspic; beef tenderloin; brioche mousseline; redcurrant jelly; Sept-Moncel cheese and fruit.]

11. *Histoire des festins insolites et de la goinfrerie,* 241. [Hors-d'oeuvres; chilled salmon; beef tenderloin; duckling; roast chicken; pheasant sausage; salad; ice cream; dessert.]

12. Auguste Escoffier, *Le guide culinaire* (1903), cited from the American edition, *The Escoffier Cookbook,* n.t. (New York: Crown Publishers, 1969), 881.

13. Jean-Bernard Naudin, Anne Borel, Alain Senderens, *Dining with Proust* (New York: Random House, 1992), 70. ["Japanese" salad; grilled crayfish; sole à la normande; salad; strawberry mousse.]

14. *Feasts of a Militant Gastronome,* 236. [Créme of Asparagus; sole à la normande; jellied beef; truffle and pineapple salad; tea sherbet; madeleines.]

15. Guillaume Apollinaire, "Le Gastro-astronomisme ou la Cuisine Nouvelle" (1912–1913), in *Le Poète assassiné* (Paris: Gallimard, 1992), 258–259. [Fresh violettes without their

stems seasoned with lemon juice; monkfish cooked in eucalyptus; rare sirloin steak seasoned with tobacco; barded quail with licorice sauce; salad seasoned with walnut oil and marc (brandy); Reblochon cheese seasoned with walnuts and nutmeg; fruit.]

16. Filippo Tommaso Marinetti and Fillìa, *La cuisine futuriste,* trans. Nathalie Heinich of *La cucina futurista* (Paris: Métailié, 1982), 153.

17. André Guillot, *La grande cuisine française* (Paris: Flammarion, 1976), 42. Guillot briefly served as a chef's aide in Roussel's household.

18. Marie-Christine Clément and Didier Clément, *Colette Gourmande* (Paris: Albin Michel, 1990), 75. [Oysters; coulibiac of salmon; chicken fricassée in Champagne; cream cake.]

19. Joseph Delteil, *La cuisine paléolithique* (Paris / Montpellier: Arléa / Presses du Languedoc), 29–34.

20. Ibid., 19.

21. Ibid., 21.

22. Lobster salad with mango and basil; Loire salmon with caviar; lamb with garlic sauce; traditional black-currant, raspberry, and wild-strawberry cakes.

23. It is thanks to the cuisine of Michel Bras—whose work is brilliantly represented in *Le Livre de Michel Bras* (Rodez: Éditions du Rouergue, 1991)—that I have begun to combine my passions for food and gardens in studies of their intricate interrelations. See Allen S. Weiss, *Unnatural Horizons: Paradox and Contradiction in Landscape Architecture* (New York: Princeton Architectural Press, 1998), 133–137. ["Gargouillou" of young vegetables with sprouts and country herbs; monkfish poached in butter with chanterelles and a sauce of butter and the frothy "skin" of fresh milk; sauteed foie gras and cabbage with chives, bacon, orange, and flower (Para) stamens; sugar peas in a bouillon made of their pods in a truffle cream sauce; grilled pigeon breast with a lemon paste and young leeks; aligot (a traditional Aubrac dish of whipped po-

tatoes, fresh Laguiole cheese, and garlic); Laguiole cheeses and blue cheeses; warm biscuit filled with liquid chocolate, with white and black sauces; applesauce in a gentian leaf with black-currants and red-currants rolled in sugar; caramel and almond dry cake with preserved cherries and wild thyme.]

24. Snail tempura accompanied with conserved tomatoes and gnocci made of aged Cantal cheese; sweetbreads with coffee beans; lobster in three servings: coral in jelly; poached claws; roast tail; flavored ices and cream-cheese with saffron on a meringue.

25. Jean-Georges Vongerichten, *Simple Cuisine* (New York: Prentice-Hall, 1990), 191.

26. The most famous book on wild, edible, indigenous American plants is Euell Gibbons, *Stalking the Wild Asparagus* (New York: David McKay Co., 1962), though it must be said that this author's sensibility is part of the vast heritage, literary and otherwise, of Henry David Thoreau's *Journals.*

27. Cited in Jean-Robert Pitte, *Gastronomie française : Histoire et géographie d'une passion* (Paris: Fayard, 1991), 196.

28. This movement has been highly publicized; see, for example, Jacques Teyssier, "Et si la haute cuisine française s'ouvrait enfin sur le monde?," in *Humanité,* 18 March 1998, which includes the group's charter.

# Select Bibliography


Aron, Jean-Paul. *The Art of Eating in France: Manners and Menus in the Nineteenth Century.* Trans. N. Rootes. London: Owen, 1975.

———. *Le mangeur du XIX$^{e}$ siècle.* 1973. Reprint, Paris, Denoël/Gonthier, 1976.

Bart, Jean, and Wahl, Élisabeth, eds. *Le vin.* Special issue of *Dix-Huitième Siècle* 29. Paris: Presses Universitaires de France, 1997.

Baudelaire, Charles. *Paradis artificiels.* 1860. In *Oeuvres complètes,* Vol. 1. Paris. Gallimard / Pléiade, 1975.

Bernier, Georges. *Antonin Carême.* Paris: Grasset, 1989.

Bonnet, Jean-Claude, and Fink, Béatrice, eds. *Aliments et cuisine.* Special issue of *Dix-Huitième Siècle* 15. Paris: Garnier, 1983.

Bras, Michel. *Le Livre de Michel Bras.* Rodez: Éditions du Rouergue, 1991.

Brillat-Savarin, Jean-Anthelme. *Physiologie du goût.* 1826. Reprint, Paris: Flammarion, 1982.

———. *The Physiology of Taste.* Trans. M. F. K. Fisher. New York: Harcourt, Brace, Jovanovich, 1978.

Camporesi, Piero. *Exotic Brew: The Art of Living in the Age of Enlightenment.* Trans. Christopher Woodall. Cambridge: Polity Press, 1998.

———. *The Magic Harvest: Food, Folklore, and Society.* Trans. J. K. Hall. Cambridge: Polity Press, 1993.

Capatti, Alberto. *Le goût du nouveau : Origines de la modernité alimentaire.* Paris: Albin Michel, 1989.

de Certeau, Michel, Giard, Luce, and Mayol, Pierre. *L'invention du quotidien : Habiter, cuisiner.* Paris: Gallimard / Folio, 1994.

Chatelain-Courtois, Martine. *Les mots du vin et de l'ivresse.* Paris: Belin, 1984.

Châtelet, Noëlle. *Le corps à corps culinaire.* 1977. Reprint, Paris: Le Seuil, 1998.

Clément, Didier, and Clément, Marie-Christine. *Colette gourmande.* Paris: Albin Michel, 1990.

Corbin, Alain. *Le miasme et la jonquille.* Paris: Flammarion / Champs, 1986.

Courtine, Robert. *Feasts of a Militant Gastronome.* Trans. June Guicharnaud. New York: William Morrow & Co., 1974.

Daudet, Marthe (Pampille). *Pampille's Table.* Trans. Shirley King. London: Faber & Faber, 1996.

Delteil, Joseph. *La cuisine paléolithique.* Paris / Montpellier: Arléa / Presses du Languedoc, 1990.

Desbiolles, Maryline. *La seiche.* Paris: Le Seuil, 1998.

———. *The Cuttlefish.* Trans. Mara Bertelsen. New York: Herodias, 2001.

Detienne, Marcel. *Les jardins d'Adonis.* Paris: Gallimard, 1972.

Dumas, Alexandre. *Mon dictionnaire de cuisine.* 1870. Reprint, Paris: Union Générale d'Éditions, 1998.

Escoffier, Auguste. *The Escoffier Cookbook.* 1903. Reprint, New York: Crown, 1969.

Fink, Béatrice. *Les liaisons savoureuses.* Saint-Étienne: l'Université de Saint-Étienne, 1995.

Fisher, M. F. K. *The Art of Eating.* New York: Vintage, 1976.

———. *With Bold Knife and Fork.* New York: Perigee Books, 1969.

Fischler, Claude. *L'Homnivore.* Paris: Odile Jacob, 1990.

Flandrin, Jean-Louis. *Chronique de Platine : Pour une histoire gastronomique.* Paris: Odile Jacob, 1992.

Flandrin, Jean-Louis, and Montanari, Massimo, eds. *Histoire de l'Alimentation.* Paris: Fayard, 1997.

Garrier, Gilbert. *Histoire sociale et culturelle du vin.* Paris: Bordas, 1996.

Gillet, Philippe. *Le goût et les mots: Littérature et gastronomie (XIVe–XXe siècles).* Paris: Payot, 1993.

———. *Par mets et par vins : Voyages et gastronomie en Europe (16e–18e siècles).* Paris: Payot, 1985.

Goody, Jack. *Cooking, Cuisine, and Class.* Cambridge: Cambridge University Press, 1982.

Grimod de la Reynière, Alexandre-Balthazar-Laurent. *Écrits gastronomiques.* Ed. Jean-Claude Bonnet. Paris: Union Générale d'Éditions, 1978.

———. *Manuel des Amphitryons.* 1808. Reprint, Paris: Métaillié, 1983.

Huysmans, Joris-Karl. *À Rebours.* 1891. Reprint, Paris: Gallimard / Folio, 1977.

Lévi-Strauss, Claude. *Le cru et le cuit.* Paris: Plon, 1964.

Lévi-Strauss, Claude. *L'origine des manières de table.* Paris: Plon, 1968.

Lu, Wenfu. *Vie et passion d'un gastronome chinois.* [1982]. Trans. Philippe Picquier. Paris: Éditions Picquier—UNESCO, 1996.

MacDonogh, Giles. *Brillat-Savarin : The Judge and His Stomach.* Chicago: Ivan R. Dee, 1992.

Naudin, Jean-Bernard, Borrel, Anne, and Senderens, Alain. *Dining with Proust.* New York: Random House, 1992.

Pitte, Jean-Robert. *Gastronomie française : Histoire et géographie d'une passion.* Paris: Fayard, 1991.

Proust, Marcel. *Du côté de chez Swann.* 1913. Reprint, Paris: Gallimard / Folio 1987.

Reboul, J.-B. *La cuisinière provençale.* 1897. Reprint, Marseille: Ruat et Tacussel, 1998.

Revel, Jean-François. *Culture and Cuisine: A Journey Through the History of Food.* Trans. Helen R. Lane. New York: Da Capo, 1984.

———. *Un festin en paroles: Histoire littéraire de la sensibilité gastronomique de l'Antiquité à nos jours.* Paris: Éditions Suger, 1985.

Romi. *Histoire des festins insolites et de la goinfrerie.* Paris: Éditions Artulen, 1993.

Rouff, Marcel. *La vie et la passion de Dodin-Bouffant, gourmet.* 1924. Reprint, Paris: Stock, 1984.

Scapp, Ron, and Seitz, Bryan, eds. *Eating Culture.* Albany: State University of New York Press, 1998.

Schehr, Lawrence R., and Weiss, Allen S., eds. *French Food: On the Table, On the Page, and in French Culture.* New York: Routledge, 2001.

Schivelbusch, Wolfgang. *Tastes of Paradise: A Social History of Spices, Stimulants, and Intoxicants.* New York: Vintage, 1993.

Serres, Michel. *Les cinq sens.* Paris: Hachette, 1985.

Spang, Rebecca. *The Invention of the Restaurant: Paris and Modern Gastronomic Culture.* Cambridge, MA: Harvard Unversity Press, 2000.

Tannahill, Reay. *Food in History.* New York: Three Rivers Press, 1989.

Tendret, Lucien. *La Table au pays de Brillat-Savarin.* Belley: Bailley, 1892.

Thorne, John, with Thorne, Matt Lewis. *Outlaw Cook.* (New York: Farrar, Straus, Giroux, 1992).

———. *Pot on the Fire.* (New York: Farrar, Straus, Giroux, 2000).

Toussaint-Samat, Maguelonne. *Histoire naturelle et morale de la nourriture.* Paris: Bordas, 1987.

Trager, James. *The Food Chronology.* New York: Henry Holt, 1995.

Visser, Margaret. *The Rituals of Dinner: The Origins, Evolution, Eccentricities, and Meaning of Table Manners.* New York: Penguin, 1991.

Weiss, Allen S. *Flamme et festin : Une poétique de la cuisine.* Paris: Éditions Java, 1994.

———, ed. *Taste, Nostalgia.* New York: Lusitania Press, 1997.

Wheaton, Barbara. *Savoring the Past: The French Kitchen and Table from 1300 to 1789.* Philadelphia: The University of Pennsylvania Press, 1983.

# About the Author

Allen S. Weiss has written and edited over twenty-five books, including *The Aesthetics of Excess* (SUNY); *Perverse Desire and the Ambiguous Icon* (SUNY); *Phantasmic Radio* (Duke); *Sade and the Narrative of Transgression* (Cambridge); *Taste, Nostalgia* (Lusitania); *Unnatural Horizons: Paradox and Contradiction in Landscape Architecture* (PAP); *Experimental Sound and Radio* (MIT); *French Food* (Routledge); and *Breathless: Sound Recording, Disembodiment, and the Transformation of Lyrical Nostalgia* (Wesleyan). He has recently directed *Theater of the Ears,* a play for electronic marionette and taped voice based on the writings of Valère Novarina, and is completing a book of short stories, *The Aphoristic Theater.* He teaches in the Departments of Performance Studies and Cinema Studies at New York University.

# Index